WHAT NOW, ADAM? THE BOOK OF MEN

Revised edition

Cover design with an image by Mattias Carson / Alamy

The text excerpts in this book are selected from various talks by Osho, given to a live audience. All of Osho's talks have been published in full as books, and are also available as original audio recordings. Audio recordings and the complete text archive can be found via the online OSHO Library at www.osho.com/library

OSHO MEDIA INTERNATIONAL
New York • Zurich • Mumbai
an imprint of
OSHO INTERNATIONAL
www.osho.com/oshointernational

Distributed by Publishers Group Worldwide
www.pgw.com

Library of Congress Catalog-In-Publication Data is available

Printed in India by Manipal Techonologies Limited, Karnataka

ISBN: 978-1-938755-42-2
This title is also available in eBook format ISBN 978-0-88050-082-1

what now, **adam?**

The Book of Men

THE CRISIS OF MANHOOD AS AN OPPORTUNITY FOR SELF-DISCOVERY

OSHO

Contents

Preface

You are fortunate to be alive today, because something immensely great is going to happen – and that is the meeting of science and religion, the meeting of West and East, the meeting of the extrovert mind and the introvert mind. It will create the new man who will be able to move easily to the outside or into the inside, who will be able to move easily into the extrovert world of science and into the introvert world of religion – just as you move outside your house into the garden and back into the house. It is not a problem, you don't need any reconciliation. Each time you come out of your house onto the lawn you need not make great effort – you simply come out. It is feeling cold inside, and the sun is beautiful and warm outside, you come onto the lawn, you sit on the lawn. Later on when it becomes too hot you simply move in because there is coolness inside.

Just as easily as you come out of your house and go in, a total man will be able to move into science and religion; the inner and outer will both be his.

Carl Gustav Jung has divided human beings into two: the extroverts and the introverts. His categorization is relevant for the past but will be utterly useless for the future, because the future man will be both together. In the past, we have always been categorizing in this way, but the future man will not be a man and will not be a woman. I am not saying biologically – biologically the woman will be a woman, and the man will be a man. But spiritually, the future man will have as many feminine qualities as the woman, and the woman will have as many masculine qualities as the man. Spiritually, they will never be labeled as man or woman anymore. And that will be the real liberation – not only the liberation of women, but the liberation of men too – liberation from straitjackets, liberation from imprisoning categories, liberation from all labels.

Man is not going to be Hindu, Mohammedan, Christian; man is not going to be Indian, German, English; man is not going to be white or black. Not that colors will disappear – the white man will be white and the black will be black – but these will become irrelevant, trivial, meaningless, they will not be decisive. The new man will have a universal consciousness, and the foundation will be laid by the meeting of science and religion.

Osho

Introduction

Men's liberation has not happened yet. Not only women, but men also need a great liberation movement – liberation from the past, from the slavery of life-negating values and social conditionings that have been imposed upon humankind by all the religions for thousands of years. Priests and politicians have created a guilt-ridden man who is alienated from himself, fighting a permanent inner war that pervades all areas of his life – a conflict between body and soul, matter and mind, materialism and spirituality, science and religion, man and woman, West and East.

Every man, from his early childhood, is being conditioned to function and survive in an efficiency-oriented, competitive world, and he is pressured from the moment he enters school to join the ambitious struggle and race for money, success, fame, power, respectability, and social status. As a small child already he learns to adopt the goals and values of his parents and teachers, his peers and those set up by the society as "role models," without ever questioning them. Thus he becomes distracted from his true nature, his original being, and he loses the capacity for unmotivated joy, childlike innocence, and playful creativity. He is cut off from his creative potential, his ability to love, his laughter, his lust for life. Before long, his senses are deadened and his emotional life is repressed. He loses access to his own innate feminine qualities of feeling, gentleness, love, and intuition, and becomes a head-oriented, efficient, unfeeling robot.

Society teaches boys to grow up to become "strong men," to suppress their feminine qualities of softness and receptivity, love and compassion. But, as Osho points out in this book, every man also has an "inner woman" within, just as every woman has an "inner man" inside. And only when these suppressed parts of ourselves are acknowledged, reclaimed, honored, can we finally become whole and fully alive.

The transforming power of meditation and awareness is an invaluable ally in this journey of becoming whole, a mature individual. Meditation is the catalyst that sets in motion and accelerates the process of inner growth. Meditation brings light to the darkness, makes us integrated, creates a balance between our male and female parts. It teaches us to live and enjoy our life in its multidimensionality – in a healthy balance of body, mind and soul, of the material and the spiritual, of the outer and inner world.

Man today is at a crossroads. In view of the multidimensional global crisis of our planet, in the beginning days of the third millennium, the question arises: "What now, Adam?" The limits of growth have long been reached, the belief in unlimited scientific and social progress, with its unending exploitation of the resources of Mother Earth, has been fundamentally shattered. All outer revolutions have failed. The time has come for an inner revolution.

Unless the individual man starts to come out of his robot-like, mechanical functioning and unawareness and begins to live his life with self-love, awareness, and deep respect for his real nature, there seems to be no chance that our world can escape global suicide.

"Man needs a new psychology to understand himself," says Osho. And the basic understanding that needs to be deeply imbibed and experienced is that "No man is just man, and no woman is just woman: each man is both man and woman, and so is each woman – woman and man. Adam has Eve in him, and Eve has Adam in her. In fact, nobody is just Adam and nobody is just Eve: we are Adam-Eves. This is one of the greatest insights ever attained."

He goes on to say:

"My vision of the new man is of a rebel, of a man who is in search of his original self, of his original face. A man who is ready to drop all masks, all pretensions, all hypocrisies, and show to the world what he, in reality, is. Whether he is loved or condemned, respected, honored or dishonored, crowned or crucified, does not matter; because to be yourself is the greatest blessing in existence."

The editors

Part 1

ADAM

Rebellion means dropping the whole past and living in the present without any tradition, without any mind, without any knowledge; living like a child, as if you are the first man, you are Adam. That is rebellion.

Adam really rebelled – even against God he rebelled. He must have been a beautiful man. He was the first man, but still, one thing that he did of tremendous importance was that he rebelled. He rebelled against an unjust order from God; it was unfair. He did not obey. And it is good: if he had obeyed, we would not be here at all. We are here because he disobeyed. We owe that much to Adam – and more particularly to Eve. That's why I have so much respect for women: it is really my respect for Eve. And I have even more respect for the serpent. He was the first enlightened person, the serpent that persuaded Eve and triggered a great rebellion.

Adam is man, and every man is Adam-like. Every childhood is in the Garden of Eden. Every child is as happy as the animals, as happy as the primitive, as happy as the trees. Have you watched a child running in the trees, on the beach? – he is not yet human. His eyes are still clear, but unconscious. He will have to come out of the Garden of Eden. That is the meaning of Adam's expulsion from the Garden of Eden – he is no longer part of the unconscious bliss. He has become conscious by eating the fruit of the tree of knowledge. He has become man.

It is not that Adam was once expelled; every Adam has to be expelled, again and again. Every child has to be thrown out of God's garden; it is part of growth. The pain is that of growth. One has to lose it to gain it again, to gain it consciously. That is man's burden and his destiny, his anguish and his freedom, man's problem and man's grandeur both.

The First Man

Until the Jews and Arabs and other tribes brought their racially exclusive and jealous God to the West, Toamy, Bacchus, Mithros and Apollo were the gods that man worshipped. Diana had her bow and arrow, Thor was in the north, the mother goddess was worshipped in the West. And then death and resurrection became the religion of the West. Guilt and sin were taught. Why is Adam a sinner? Why isn't he like Theseus or Jason or Hermes? Is the concept of sin just a trick? To make men meditate?

I am a pagan. There is no God for me, except this existence. God is intrinsic to life. God is not outside life, God is this very life. To live this life totally is to live a divine life. To live this life partially is to live an undivine life. To be partial is to be irreligious. To be total and whole is to be holy.

The questioner asks about the past. In the past, all over the world, people were pagans, simple nature worshippers. There was no concept of sin, there was no question of guilt. Life was accepted as it is. There was no evaluation, no interpretation – reason had not interfered yet.

The moment reason starts interfering, condemnation comes. The moment reason enters, division, split starts, and man becomes schizophrenic. Then you start condemning something in your being – one part becomes higher, another part becomes lower, and you lose balance.

But this had to happen; reason had to come, this is part of

growth. As it happens to every child, it had to happen to the whole of humanity, too. When the child is born he is a pagan; each child is a born pagan. He is happy the way he is. He has no idea what is right and what is wrong; he has no ideals. He has no criteria, he has no judgment. Hungry, he asks for food. Sleepy, he falls asleep. That's what Zen masters say is the uttermost in religion – when hungry eat, when feeling sleepy go to sleep. Let life flow; don't interfere.

Each child is born as a pagan, but sooner or later he will lose that simplicity. That is part of it; that has to happen, it is part of our growth, maturity, destiny. The child has to lose it and find it again. When the child loses it he becomes the ordinary man, the worldly man. When he regains it he becomes religious.

The child's innocence is very cheap: it is a gift from God, he has not earned it. He will have to lose it – only by losing it will he become aware of what he has lost. Then he will start searching for it. And only when he searches for it, and earns it, achieves it, becomes it – then he will know the tremendous preciousness of it.

What happens to a sage? He becomes a child again; nothing else happens to a sage. He is again innocent. He went into the world of reason, division, ego, a thousand and one ideals; he went almost mad with evaluation. And then one day, finding it all just absurd, stupid, he drops it. But this second childhood is far more valuable than the first childhood. The first childhood was just given to you. You were not even asked, it was a pure gift. And we cannot value gifts; you value a thing only when you make effort for it, when you strive for it, and when it takes a long journey to come to it.

There is a Sufi story:

A man, a seeker, came to a Sufi mystic. And he asked, "I am searching for my master. Sir, I have heard you are a wise man. Can you tell me the characteristics of a master? How am I to judge? Even if I find my master, how am I going to decide that he is my master? I am a blind man; I am ignorant, I don't know anything about it. And without finding a master, it is said, no one can find God. So I am in search for a master. Help me."

The Sufi mystic told him a few things. He said, "These are the characteristics. You will find the master in such a way, with such a behavior, and he will be sitting under such a tree. And he will be wearing such a robe, and his eyes will be like this."

The seeker thanked the old man and went in search. Thirty years passed, and the man roamed almost all over the world, but he could not find the man who was his master according to the old man's description. Tired, exhausted, frustrated, he comes back to his home town and sees the old man. The old man has become very old, but the moment the seeker comes near, he sees. The old man is sitting under the same tree – suddenly he sees this is the tree the old man had talked about. And this is the robe the old man had described, and these are the eyes, and this is the silence that the old man had described. This is the benediction in the presence of the master.

He is overjoyed, but a great question also arises in his mind. He bows down, touches the master's feet, and says, "Before I surrender to you, just tell me why you tortured me for these thirty years. Why didn't you tell me right then, 'I am your master'?"

The old man started laughing and he said, "I told you that he will be sitting under such a tree – and this is the tree I was sitting under! And I told you, 'This will be the robe he will be wearing' – and I was wearing the same robe! I was the same man then, but you were not alert. You could not see me – you needed this thirty years' journey from one corner to another corner of the world; you needed all this effort to recognize me. I was here, but you were not here.

"Now you are also here, you can see me. And I had to wait for you. It is not only a question for you, that you have been traveling. Think of me! I am so old, and I could not even die before you came back. And I have not changed my robe, in case you missed me again – for thirty years, I have never for a single moment left this tree! But you have come. The journey has been too long – but this is the way one discovers."

God is always here, but we are not here. A child has to lose track; he has to go for thirty years' pilgrimage. Every child has to lose track, every child has to go astray. Only by going astray, only by suffering will he attain eyes, clarity, transparency. Only by going into a thousand and one things will he start looking for the real.

The unreal has to be explored. The unreal is attractive, the unreal is magnetic. And how can you know the real if you have not known the unreal? The child knows the real, but he has not known the unreal so he cannot define the real. The child knows God – but he has not known the world, so he cannot define God. Each child comes like a saint but has to become a sinner; then the second childhood.

If you don't attain the second childhood you have missed your life. So don't think, and don't be worried, that you have lost it. Everybody has to lose it – that should not be a problem. The problem is only if you go on and on, and you never come back. If this man goes on and on – thirty years, thirty lives, three hundred lives, three thousand lives – goes on and on, and never comes back, and never attains the second childhood, then something has really gone wrong.

Err – to err is human; that is the way to learn. Go astray – going astray is the way to come back home. Forget God, so that you can remember him. Escape from God, so one day the thirst becomes a fire in you and you have to come to God again like a hungry man, like a thirsty man.

This had to happen to humanity too. Now there will be a great assertion of paganism in the world again – the second childhood. That's why Zen has become so important, so significant; Tantra has become such a significant word. Sufism, Hasidism are more important now than Christianity, Islam, Hinduism, Buddhism, Jainism – why? Why Tantra? Why Tao? Why Zen? Why Sufi? Why Hasid? These are the pagan attitudes – they create the second childhood.

The world is getting ready; humanity is becoming more and more mature. This age is the age of humanity's youth. The childhood is no more; we have lost it, we have become corrupted. But don't be worried by it – that is how one attains innocence again. And the second childhood is far more valuable than the first, because the second cannot be lost. The first has to be lost, is bound to be lost. No child, not even a buddha, could retain it. No child can retain it; it is in the very nature of things. When something is given to you and you were not seeking it, were not even asking for it, you were not ready even to receive it...

If you give a child a diamond, a diamond like the Kohinoor, he will play with it a little while and then throw it away. He does not know what it is. The Kohinoor is the Kohinoor, whether you know it or not. The Kohinoor is the Kohinoor – knowledge makes no difference. But the child will throw it away. He will become fed up sooner or later: just a stone... How long can you play with it? Even if it is very colorful, even if it is very shiny, but how long?

For the Kohinoor to come into your life again, you will need a thirst for it. You will need to feel a great missing – something missing inside your being. You will need a great desire. All desires should become lesser desires, and God becomes the supreme-most desire, the topmost desire. God is always here.

It happens to children, it happens to societies, it happens to civilizations, it happens to humanity at large, too. So don't be worried about Christianity – that was part. Christianity or those kinds of religion are the religions between these two childhoods, the first and the second. They condemn. They shout that you have gone astray: "Come back!" They pull you back, they make you afraid. They give you great provocations, that if you come back you will attain great prizes, rewards in heaven. If you don't come back, you are going to be thrown into hell. Hellfire is waiting for you; for eternity you will be in hell, suffering. This is fear – creating fear in people so that they will come back. But out of fear, even if you come back you never come. Because fear can never become love. Fear cannot be reduced into love, cannot be converted into love. Fear remains fear, and out of fear arises hatred.

That's why Christianity has created great hatred against religion. Friedrich Nietzsche is a by-product of Christianity; if Friedrich Nietzsche says God is dead, it is just a reaction to Christianity. Too much emphasis on God, on heaven and hell – somebody has to say it. I am all for Nietzsche – somebody has to say, "Enough is enough. Stop all this nonsense! God is dead, and man is free" – because man feels in bondage if you create fear.

And greed? Greed again is a bondage. You just see – heaven, paradise, *firdaus*, the idea of it – what is it? It is such greed, such lust. In heaven it seems saints are doing nothing but copulating. Beautiful women are available and streams of wine are flowing, and all that you need is immediately made available. And those beautiful women remain at the age of sixteen; they never grow.

And one more beautiful thing about that: they again become virgin. Whenever a saint makes love to a woman – only saints go there – when a saint makes love to a woman, the moment he is finished, again she becomes a virgin. That is the miracle of paradise. And what are your saints doing there? It seems an orgy, sexual orgy! And streams of wine... Here you say, "Avoid wine, avoid women" – for what? To gain better women and more wine in heaven? This seems to be illogical.

But this is how people are provoked, through greed, to come back into the fold. Or fear: if you don't come through greed, then fear, then hellfire – and eternal hellfire! You have not done so much sin, eternal hellfire is unjust. Okay, for ten years you are thrown into hell, one can understand – fifteen years, twenty years, fifty years. But eternal? You have not been eternally sinning here, so how can eternal punishment be given to you? It looks too much.

But that is not the point; the point is just to make people afraid. Fear and greed have been the base of many religions. And they have not been helpful; they have destroyed. They have not appealed to the courageous, they have appealed only to the cowards – and when a cowardly person becomes religious, the religion is bogus. Because a cowardly person cannot become religious; only a courageous person can become religious – religion needs great courage.

It is a jump into the unknown. It is a jump into the uncharted sea, with no maps. It is dropping the past and moving into the future, it is going into insecurity. It cannot be out of cowardice.

In your temples and in your mosques, in your churches, cowards have gathered together. They are trembling with fear. And they are full of greed – afloat in greed, aflame with greed, agog with greed. These greedy and cowardly people cannot be religious. The basis of religion is to drop all fear and to drop all greed, and to move into the unknown. God is the unknown, the hidden. He is hidden here – in the trees, in the rocks, in you, in me. But to enter that hidden reality, that occult, one needs great courage – it is going into a dark night without any light.

A Zen master was saying good-bye to one of his disciples, and the night was very dark. The disciple was a little bit afraid, scared, because he had to pass through a jungle of at least ten miles. And it was wild. Wild animals were there, and it was night – a dark night with no moon. And it was getting late, almost half the night had passed. Talking to the master, he had completely forgotten.

Seeing him a little afraid, the master says, "You look a little afraid, so I will give you a lamp." He puts a small paper lamp into his hand, lights the lamp. The disciple thanks him, goes down the steps, and the master calls him and says, "Stop!" And the master comes close and blows the flame out. And he says, "A real master gives courage; he does not help cowardice. Go into the dark, be your own light. And remember, nobody else's light will be of any help; you will have to attain your own light. Be a flame to your own being. Go into the dark, be courageous."

He says a real master never helps any cowardice. In a small act, by blowing the flame out, the master gives a great message: Religion is only for the courageous.

Those who followed Jesus, they were courageous people. They were not many, they were very few – you could have counted them on your fingers. Those who followed Buddha were courageous people. Christians are not courageous, Buddhists are not courageous. Those who are with me are courageous people. Once I am gone, your children and your children's children may pay their respect to me, but they will not be courageous.

Religion exists only when there is an alive master to live it for you. When the master is gone then religion becomes dead. Cowardly people gather together around a dead religion; then there is no fear. They worship the scripture, they worship the word, they worship the statue – all dead things. But whenever a Jesus is there, or a Buddha is there, or a Mohammed is there, they are very much afraid. They find a thousand and one ways to escape; they find a thousand and one ways to rationalize their escape. They condemn the real master – why? The real master will not support your cowardice. He will not give you any more greed – you already have too much – and he will not make you afraid. His whole effort will be to take fear and greed away from you, so that you can become capable of living your life in totality.

Christianity and religions like that had to happen. They have to be forgiven; don't be angry about them. But now they have to go too – now the world is no longer in need of them. They are tumbling, they are scattering, they are dying. In fact they are dead. But people are so blind that for them to know that their church or their temple is dead takes such a long time. They are so unconscious, they cannot understand it immediately. Christianity is dead, Hinduism dead. In Islam, only a small thing lives, still has a flame – that is Sufism. In Christianity, only a few mystics are still alive. Otherwise the church and the pope and the Vatican are just cemeteries, graveyards.

In Hinduism, a few mystics are still alive – a Krishnamurti, somewhere a Raman Maharshi – but far and few in between. Otherwise, the shankaracharyas are dead people. But nobody goes to a living master. In Buddhism only Zen is alive; in Judaism only Hasidism is alive.

The organized religion is not the real religion. The unorganized, the rebellious, the unorthodox, the heretic religion is the real religion

– has always been so. Religion comes always as a rebellion – its very spirit is that of rebelliousness. The days for organized religions are gone. In the future, a totally different kind of religion, a different kind of climate, will surround the earth. Religions will disappear; there will only be a kind of religiousness. People will find their own religion individually; people will find their own prayer, their own way of praying. There is no need to follow anybody's prescribed idea – that is not the path, that is not the way of the courageous. That is the way of the coward.

And God is available – you just have to become courageous to look into his eyes.

You ask me: "And then death and resurrection became the religion of the West." That's true. Christianity has never been concerned with Christ; it has been more concerned with the cross. It has not worshipped Christ, it has been worshipping the cross. The cross is a symbol of death. Why? Because death is the basic fear. Making people alert about their death makes them afraid. If you make a person very much mindful of death, every possibility is there that he will start shaking and trembling. And when a person is shaking and trembling you can victimize him very easily; you can convert him into any nonsense. He is ready to believe anything – if you just promise immortality he is ready.

So followers of Christianity say, "Those who are in the church will be saved, and those who are not in the church, we don't make any guarantee for them. They are doomed; they cannot be saved." And that's what all other religions say. This is creating fear. Bring death into their mind, they become afraid – who will not become afraid of death? And then an afraid man is prone to be converted into a slave very easily.

And why resurrection? Death and resurrection became the foundation of Christianity in the West. Death gives you fear, and the promise of resurrection gives you greed. If you die within the church, you will resurrect. You will resurrect as a divine being, with all that you always wanted, with all that you always needed – beautiful, with a golden body, with an aura around you, you will be resurrected.

These are fear–greed tricks, punishment–reward tricks. This is what B. F. Skinner goes on doing with his rats: make them afraid and they start doing things. This is what you see in a circus: make the elephant afraid – such a courageous animal and such a wise animal, but just make him afraid. And he starts doing foolish things for you: he will sit on a stool, he will bow down to a man – he can kill that man within a second. Even lions, seeing the whip, tremble – just make them afraid, that's all. Even lions can be tamed, and elephants can be taught and disciplined. Create fear and reward – if the elephant follows you, give him good food; if he does not follow, starve him. A simple technique.

That's what so-called religions have been doing to man. Guilt and sin were taught. Naturally, if you want to make people afraid – and that is the only way to exploit them – teach them that everything is sin, all that you enjoy is sin. Death creates fear, but death is far away. After fifty years or seventy years you will die – who bothers? "Seventy years? We will see. Right now we are not dying."

Maybe old people become afraid. That's why you find more old people in churches, temples. Old women, old men – women more than men, because they become more afraid. Old, dying, just on the verge, so they know now something has to be done. Life is going, slipping by; they have to manage something for the future.

Do you see young people in your churches? In your temples? And remember, wherever you see young people, there religion is alive. A young person, if he becomes interested in religion, his religion cannot be that of fear and cannot be that of death. His religion will be of life.

Many times people come to me and they say, "Why do so many young people come to you?" They come because I teach the religion of life, of love, of joy. I don't create any guilt, and I don't go on conditioning their minds: "This is sin, that is sin." There are mistakes, but there is no sin. Mistakes, certainly, there are – but a mistake is a mistake. If you are doing a mathematical problem and you make two plus two equal five, is it a sin? It is just a mistake; it can be corrected. No need to throw you in hell forever just because you counted two plus two as five. It is simply a mistake, pardonable.

All that you call sin is nothing but mistakes. And mistakes are the way of learning. Those people who never commit mistakes are the most stupid people because they never grow. I teach you: go on committing mistakes, never be afraid. Just remember one thing – don't commit the same mistake again and again because that is meaningless. Be inventive, commit new mistakes every day – then you learn. Just don't commit the same mistake every day because that is foolish. You have committed it once, you have known it is a mistake – you were angry, and you have seen what anger is – now being angry again is stupid. You have seen, it is just meaningless. It is destructive – it destroys the other, it destroys you. And it does not bring anything; no flower flowers in you.

You become less by anger, you don't become more. Love, be kind – and suddenly you are more flowing, bigger, higher; you start floating, you have less weight. So learn: when you love, when you are loving, you can fly; wings grow. When you hate, when you are angry, you become like a rock. Then gravitation is too much on you, you become heavy.

Can't you see that? Simple – just like two plus two is four. Life is a learning, it is a school. That's why we have been sent here, that is the purpose – not to punish you. I would like to change your whole idea about it. You have been taught that you have been sent here to be punished – this is absolutely wrong. You are sent here to learn.

Why should God be such a torturer? Is he a sadist or something? He enjoys torturing people? And if, as these people say, you have been sent here to be punished, then why were you sent the first time? There must have been your first life – before that you had not committed anything, because how can you commit sins unless you come here? You cannot have committed any sins – then why were you sent for the first time?

They don't have any answer for why man has been sent. Maybe this time you have been sent because in the past life you committed sins. Okay, but what about the first life? And if this is the first life, as Christians say, then why have you been sent here? Now, they have a very absurd idea: because Adam committed sin. You have nothing to do with Adam; this is simply absurd. Somebody – you don't know whether he ever even existed or not – committed sin and the whole humanity is suffering for it. Your father committed sin and you have been sent to jail. And Adam is not even your father – not even your father's father, not even your father's father's father – he is the first man.

And what he has done does not seem to be a sin at all. It seems simple courage, it seems simple rebelliousness. Each child needs that much spine. God said to Adam, "Don't eat the fruit of this tree. This tree is the tree of knowledge." And Adam ate it. I think anybody who has any soul would do the same. If Adam had been dead and dull, then he would have followed. He must have been challenged; in fact, that is the very purpose. Otherwise, on the earth there are millions and millions of trees – just think, if God had not shown the particular tree, it is very, very unlikely that Adam would have found it. That was only one tree in the whole garden of God, and the garden is infinite. That was only one tree of which God said particularly, "Don't eat it. If you eat the fruit of knowledge you will be expelled."

My own understanding is that God was putting a challenge to him. He was trying to see whether Adam is alive or dead. He was trying to see whether he is capable of disobeying, whether he can say no – God was trying to see whether he is just a yes-man. And Adam proved his mettle: he ate the fruit. He was ready to be thrown into the world, but he showed spirit. It is not sin, it is simply courage.

Every child has to disobey his father one day or other, every child has to disobey his mother one day or other. In fact, the day you disobey is the day you start becoming mature – never before it. So only stupid children never disobey. Intelligent children certainly disobey; intelligent children find a thousand and one ways to disobey the parents. You can look around: you will always find the intelligent child disobeying. Because he has to grow his own soul – if he goes on obeying you, obeying you, obeying you, when will he grow? How will he grow? He will remain dull and limp. He will not have his own soul, he will not have his own individuality.

No, Adam has not committed any sin; Adam is the first saint. He disobeyed God, and God wanted it. That is exactly what God wanted – that Adam should disobey. Disobeying God, Adam will go far away into the world; he will lose his first childhood. Then he will suffer many, many mistakes and from those mistakes he will learn.

And one day he will come back – as Christ, as Buddha, as Mahavira, as Krishna, he will come back.

This going away is a must for coming back. This is not against God, really, this is precisely what God wanted to happen. It was absolutely planned by God himself. So I don't call it sin. Why is Adam called a sinner? He is called a sinner because your religions depend on calling you sinners, on condemning you. The more you are condemned, the more you touch their feet. The more you are condemned, the more you crawl on the earth and beg. The more you are condemned, the more afraid you become.

The more you are afraid, the more you need mediators. You

don't know where God is. Your priest knows, your pope knows; he has a direct line with God. If the priest intervenes, only then can you be saved – otherwise your whole life is sin. Only if he persuades God for you then you can be saved. This is the whole trick, the trick of the priest. The priest is not really a religious man, the priest is a businessman – doing business in the name of religion, exploiting. The ugliest profession in the world is not of the prostitutes, the ugliest profession is of the priests.

You ask, "Why isn't he like Theseus or Jason or Hermes?" He is. "Is the concept of sin just a trick? To make men meditate?" Yes, it is a trick, but not to make them meditate. It is a trick to make them slaves. Meditation is a totally different thing. Meditation never comes out of fear; meditation comes out of understanding. Meditation comes out of love, out of compassion. Meditation comes out of living your life in all climates, in all seasons. Looking into each fact of life deeply, understanding it – and if it is meaningless discarding it, if it is meaningful choosing it – by and by, you go on collecting the essential and discarding the nonessential.

Both are there. The chaff and the wheat, both are there. The roses and the weeds, both are there. And one has to make a distinction between the chaff and the wheat: one has to throw the chaff and collect the wheat. This much intelligence is needed, otherwise you cannot become a religious person.

These fears don't give you understanding. They in fact cloud your mind more, they make you more unclear about life. They don't allow you to go into life totally and experience it – they are against experience.

Meditation comes when you live life, and you see life as it happens. Not because Buddha says anger is bad – that will not help; you will become a parrot, a pundit – but if you see into your own anger and this understanding arises, that anger is meaningless, poisonous. Not because Krishna says, "Leave everything to God, surrender to God" – no, following Krishna you will not attain God – but see how your ego is creating all kinds of miseries for you.

Seeing that, one day you drop the ego and you say, "Now I will live in a totally surrendered way. Whatever God wants through me will happen. I will not have any desire of my own, I will not have any will of my own. I drop my will."

Seeing the misery that ego brings, comes surrender. Seeing the misery that anger brings, comes love. Seeing the misery that sexuality brings, arises *brahmacharya*, celibacy. But one has to go through it – there is no shortcut, and these things cannot be borrowed from anybody.

The modern man is not suffering from his own sins, as the so-called religious preachers go on saying to you. You are suffering from the sins of centuries... But now things have come to a peak. Man is falling apart. Up to now somehow we have managed to keep ourselves together, but now things have come to such a point that either man has to change totally and has to change his vision of life, or man has to commit suicide.

If you follow the past, then you are on the verge of committing a global suicide. Just a bird's eye view and you can see the earth is preparing for a global suicide, a total destruction, a total war. And remember again, this has nothing to do with the modern man as such. The modern man is only a victim of the whole past. Unless we drop this whole pathological past and start anew, living in the present, with no idea of perfection, with no ideals, with no shoulds, with no commandments, man is doomed.

The Victim

Why do I so often think of committing suicide?

You must be intelligent. Only stupid people never think of suicide. Life is so ugly, life is such a hell. It is very difficult to find an intelligent person who never thinks of committing suicide. The more intelligent you are, the more the idea will be coming again and again: Why go on living? For what? For this same rut? – going to the office every day, doing the same files every day, coming back every day, talking about the same things, reading the same newspaper, listening to the same stupid radio station, going to sleep, just to get up early in the morning and catch the train to the office and so on and so forth, every day, year in and year out.

Only a very, very mediocre person can go on living. Otherwise, one day or other, the idea arises: "What am I doing here? If this is the way life goes, I have lived for forty years repeating the same thing; I may live forty years more, repeating the same things again, then what? Then why not stop this game? Why not return the ticket to existence and say, 'I am finished. Enough is enough!'"

The idea of suicide comes to everybody. That's why it is only man who thinks of suicide, no other animal. It is only man who ponders over the idea of suicide, and sometimes commits suicide. It simply shows intelligence and nothing else.

And particularly in the modern society, man thinks more of suicide because modern society has become more mature, more intelligent, more educated, more sophisticated. In the old days, people were not thinking of suicide so much, for many reasons. In the old days, people were not individuals. They belonged to groups, castes, religions, countries. They had no individual existence as such, and only individuals can commit suicide, remember.

When you have the idea that you are an individual, then the possibility opens up: you can destroy yourself. In the past, man has lived as part of a collective mind. And a collective mind is not a very intelligent mind. The collective mind lives according to the lowest denominator, it cannot reach to the highest peaks of understanding, of vision, of seeing. The collective mind lives in a meaningless rut, thinking that this is meaningful because everybody else is doing the same, so it must be meaningful.

The modern mind is at a loss, the meaning is lost. You have to decide your own meaning. In the old days, when a son was born to a carpenter, then he was going to become a carpenter. It was decided, already decided. His parents, his parents' parents, as far back as one could remember, they have always been carpenters. So he is a carpenter, he knows his identity, who he is. He knows what he has to do. The society prescribes every rule, every regulation; he simply has to follow it. It is living below individuality, and nobody can think of suicide when you live below individuality.

When you start becoming an individual, when you start standing on your own, then suddenly you see the point: "What is the purpose of it all? What am I doing here?"

Secondly, in the modern world, everybody has to choose his own identity. That is a great effort. And when you choose your own identity it is always with a suspicion that it may be right, it may not be right. In the old days, when a man was born to a brahmin family he knew that he was a brahmin. There was no need to think about it, it was predetermined. All was given to him as a blueprint; he just had to live it. The whole script was supplied by the society; he was just an actor in a drama.

Now the problem is more complicated. You have to write the drama, you have to create the stage, you have to find the actors. You are the director and the actor and the storywriter and the songwriter. You are the stage, and not only that, you are the audience too. How can you be absolutely certain who you are? Modern man is living continuously in what psychoanalysts call "the identity crisis."

In the old days, the authority was there to tell you what was right and what was wrong. You were not left on your own to decide.

Things were clear-cut: "This is right and that is wrong." People followed the authorities.

Now authorities have disappeared, the world is living in a kind of freedom. The more a society is free, the more people will think of suicide. The more a society is free, the more people will commit suicide.

In the East, particularly in India, the so-called religious saints feel very, very enhanced by the idea that the suicide rate in India is very low compared to America. And they think America is committing suicide because it is materialist. They are utter fools: America is committing suicide more because America has more freedom. America is more tense, in anxiety, because America is creating individuality. India is not yet that free; India still lives in the past. America is trying to live in the present and in the future, hence the problem: anguish.

America is paralyzed. Because when you have to decide on your own what is right and what is wrong, and there are no longer any absolute criteria – no Vedas, no Manu, no Moses, no Mahavira, nobody saying to you "This is right" – you have to decide on your own. Hesitation arises, confusion arises.

Freedom is always confusing. A slave lives in a relaxed way; he need not worry, whatever the master says, he follows. He has no anxiety. If it is wrong, the master is responsible. If it is right, the master knows. He is just to follow. His is not to ask why, he has to do and die. He is a mechanical robot.

I have heard, in the novel *Mother Night*, Kurt Vonnegut portrays the desperate woman Resi beseeching her lover:

"Then tell me what to live for, anything at all. It does not have to be love. Anything at all!" She gestured at objects around the shabby room, dramatizing exquisitely the sense of the world's being a junk shop. "I will live for that chair, that picture, that furnace pipe, that couch, that crack in the wall! Tell me to live for it, and I will!" she cried. "Just tell me what it should be!"

There is nobody to tell you. In the old days, everything was told to you, nothing was left to you. Parents were telling you, "Marry this woman." Astrologers were deciding that this was the right woman for you, and you were marrying a certain woman because your parents decided, the astrologer decided, your birth chart decided. You were not deciding yourself. When you were not deciding, there was no anxiety.

Now you have to decide yourself. There are millions of women in the world, whom to choose? How to decide whether this woman is going to be a heaven or a hell? There is no way to predict. One is in turmoil. A profession has to be decided on, which to choose? Religions have no more grip; a Christian does not really feel like he belongs to the church. Now all the ground underneath your feet has disappeared.

Unless you are an absolutely mediocre person, it will be very difficult for you not to think of suicide. Suicide seems to be a great release from anxiety, a release from choosing, a release from alternatives.

In the novel *Cat's Cradle*, one character says, "We doodely do, what we muddily must, until we bodily bust."

If you are a person like that, then there is no question of suicide. Intelligence thinks about whether life is worth living; intelligence never takes anything for granted. So the first thing I would like to tell you when you ask "Why do I so often think of committing suicide?" is that you are an intelligent person. Don't feel guilty; every intelligent person thinks that way. This is the beginning of intelligence, although not the end. And by committing suicide, nothing is changed. You will be born again, and the whole nonsense will start from *ABC*. That is pointless. When you are thinking of suicide, that simply says you are thinking that this life that you have lived up to now is not worth living.

But there are possibilities in it which you have not yet tried. I say to you: This life can become a great joy. It became a great joy to Krishna, it became a great ecstasy to Christ, it became a jubilation to Buddha, it is a benediction to me, why can it not be so for you?

All these people had been thinking of suicide, remember. To think of suicide is to grope for sannyas. To think of suicide simply means this life is finished, but there are other alternative lives possible. One need not destroy this beautiful gift from existence. The life that you have lived is not the only alternative. It can be lived in a thousand and one ways; there are other ways to live it.

You may have lived a life without love. Why not try love? You may have lived a life obsessed with money. Why not live a life not obsessed with money? You may have lived a life which hankers to possess. Now live a life which is not worried about possessing anything. You may have lived a life of respectability, always considering what people think about you, what their opinion is. There is a life to live without bothering what others are thinking about you; there is a life to live individually and rebelliously.

There is a life to live which is of adventure and not of social conformity. There is a life of meditation, of godliness, of search, of going within. You may have lived an outside life, chasing this and chasing that. I make available to you another life of not chasing anything, but sitting silently, disappearing within your being – a life of interiority.

And you will be surprised, the whole idea of suicide will disappear like dewdrops in the morning sun, and you will stumble upon a life which is eternal.

Albert Camus has said: "What counts is not the best living, but the most living. To two men living the same number of years, the world always provides the same sum of experiences. It is up to us to be conscious of them. Being aware of one's life, one's revolt, one's freedom, and to the maximum, is living, and to the maximum."

Become free of your so-called life that you have lived up to now. Don't commit suicide! Let your past commit suicide. Start living afresh, moment to moment. Don't live in desires, but live in a kind of desirelessness.

You have lived a life of strain, effort, struggle. Now start living a life of relaxation, calm and quiet. And you will be surprised – you have been missing life, not because life is worthless. You have been missing life because you have been taught to live a worthless kind of life.

All the cultures want the son to respect the father. Why? – because psychologically every son disrespects the father. The reasons are clear. The father is trying to mold him in a certain way that is not natural to him. The father is making him according to his own image, just as God did – he made man in his own image. Every father is doing that.

But who wants to be made by somebody else in his own image? Everybody wants to be individual. That is a very deep longing and desire in every being, to be himself, and the father is not allowing him to be himself. And the son is helpless because he is dependent for everything on the father; hence, he has to suppress himself, be obedient.

Every father wants the son to be obedient. God wanted Adam and Eve to be obedient. Their only sin was that they disobeyed the father. And the great God – who is compassion, who is love, who is forgiveness – could not forgive his own son, his own daughter? And they had not done anything so big that for thousands of years to come the dependents should also be punished.

These stories are significant. There is no God and there has never been any Adam and Eve, but the story is very psychological; it is happening every day in thousands of places.

The Son

> You have said that duty is a four-letter word, but I have also heard you say many times that you want us to be tremendously responsible. Please tell me, are not a sense of duty and a sense of responsibility the same thing?

Duty and responsibility are synonyms in the dictionary, but not in life. In life they are not only different, they are diametrically opposite. Duty is other-oriented, responsibility is self-oriented. When you say "I have to do it," it is a duty. "Because my mother is ill, I have to go and sit by her side." Or, "I have to take flowers to the hospital. I have to do it, she is my mother." Duty is other-oriented: you don't have any responsibility. You are fulfilling a social formality because she is your mother; you don't love her. That's why I say that duty is a four-letter, dirty, word. If you love your mother, you will not say "This is a duty." If you love your mother, you will go to the hospital, you will take the flowers, you will serve your mother, you will be by her bedside, you will massage her feet, you will feel for her, but it will not be a duty – it will be responsibility. You will respond out of your heart.

Responsibility means the capacity to respond. Your heart vibrates, you feel for her, you care for her – not that she is your mother, that is irrelevant – you love the woman. She is your mother – or not, that is secondary – but you love the woman, you love the woman as a person. It is a flowing from your heart. And you will not feel that you have obliged her, you will not go advertising all around that you are such a dutiful son. You will not feel that you have done something. You have not done anything. What have you done? Just taking a few flowers to the mother who is ill, and you feel that you have fulfilled a great obligation? That's why I say that *duty* is dirty. The very word is dirty; it is other-oriented.

Responsibility has a totally different dimension. You love, you care, you feel; it comes out of your feeling. Duty comes out of thinking that she is your mother – that's why. "Therefore..." – it is a syllogism, it is logical. You go somehow, dragging yourself; you would like to escape, but what can you do? Your respectability is at stake. What will people say? Your mother is ill and you are enjoying yourself in the club and you are dancing, and your mother is ill? No, your ego will be hurt. If you could avoid this mother without your respectability being affected and your ego being affected, you would like to avoid. You will go to the hospital and you will be in a hurry to rush away, you will find some reason: "I have to go, because there is an appointment." There may not be. You want to avoid this woman, you don't want to be with her, even five minutes are too much. You don't love.

Duty I am against, but responsibility – yes, I say that my sannyasins have to be tremendously responsible. And once you drop duty, you are free to be responsible.

In my childhood my grandfather used to like his feet to be massaged, and he would call anybody – whoever was passing. He was very old, and he would say, "Will you massage my feet?"

Sometimes I would say yes and I would massage, and sometimes I would say no. He became intrigued. He asked, "What is the matter? Sometimes you say yes, and nobody massages my feet as lovingly as you do – but sometimes you simply say no."

I said, "Whenever it is a duty, I say no. Whenever it is a responsibility, I do it."

He asked, "What is the difference?"

I said, "This is the difference. When I feel love, when I would like to massage your feet, then I do it. When I feel it is just a formality, because you have asked and I have to do it, my mind will not be here. Because the children are playing outside and they are inviting me...I will not be here at all; then I don't want to do it because that is ugly." So sometimes it would happen that I had to say no to him when he wanted a massage, and sometimes I would simply go to him and ask "Would you like a little massage? I am in the mood. I will really do a beautiful job. Allow me."

Do whatever comes out of your feeling, out of your heart; never repress your heart. Never follow your mind because the mind is a social byproduct; it is not your reality. Move out of your reality; function out of your reality. Don't function out of principles, etiquette, patterns of behavior, what Confucius calls "gentlemanly." Don't be a gentleman, be a man – that's enough. Be a woman – that's enough. And be truly a man, truly a woman. Sometimes you will feel like doing something; do it, pour your heart into it. It will be a beautiful flowering. Sometimes you won't want to do – say so, be clear about it. There is no need to camouflage it.

How to love my mother?

A mother has to be loved in a totally different way. She is not your beloved – and cannot be. If you become too attached to your mother you will not be able to find a beloved. And then deep down you will be angry with your mother – because it is because of her that you couldn't move to another woman. So it is part of growth that one has to move away from the parents. It is just like your being in the womb and then having to come out of it. That was leaving your mother, in a way. In a way, betraying her. But if inside the womb the child thinks that this will be a betrayal – "How can I leave my mother who has given birth to me?" – then he will kill himself and the mother also. He *has* to come out of the womb.

First he is joined with the mother completely; then the cord has to be cut. He starts breathing on his own – that is the beginning of growth. He becomes an individual, he starts functioning separately. But for many years he will still remain dependent. For milk, food, shelter, love, he will depend on the mother; he is helpless. But as he becomes stronger, he will start moving further and further away. Then the milk will stop, and then he will have to depend on some other food. Now he is going even further away.

Then one day he has to go to school, has to make friends. And when he becomes a young man he falls in love with a woman and completely forgets the mother in a way, because this new woman overwhelms him, overpowers him. If it doesn't happen then something has gone wrong. If the mother tries to cling to you she is not fulfilling her duty as a mother. It is a very delicate duty.

A mother has to help you go away – that's what makes it delicate. A mother has to make you strong so that you can go away from her. That's her love. Then she is fulfilling her duty. If you cling to the mother, then too you are doing wrong. Then it is going against nature. It is as if a river starts flowing upstream. Then everything will be topsy-turvy.

The mother is your source. If you start floating toward the mother you are going upstream. You have to move away. The river has to go away from the source to the ocean. But that doesn't mean that you are not in love with your mother.

So remember that love for the mother has to be more like respect, less like love. Love toward your mother has to be more of the quality of gratefulness, respect, deep respect. She has given you birth, she has brought you into the world. Your love has to be very, very prayerful toward her. So do whatever you can do to serve her. But don't make your love like the love for a beloved; otherwise you are confusing your mother with the beloved. And when goals are confused *you* will become confused. So remember well that your destiny is to find a lover – another woman, not your mother. Then only for the first time will you become perfectly mature, because finding another woman means that now you are completely cut away from the mother; the final cord has been cut now.

That's why there is a subtle antagonism between the mother and the wife of her son; a very subtle antagonism, all over the world. It has to be so, because the mother feels somehow that this woman has taken her son away from her. And that's natural in a way – natural, but ignorant. The mother should be happy that some other woman has been found. Now her child is no longer a child; he has become a mature, grown-up person. She should be happy, mm?

So you can be mature only in one way – if you go away from the mother. And this is so on many levels of being. A son has some day to revolt against the father – not without respect, with deep respect. But one has to revolt. This is where one needs to be delicate: revolution is there, rebellion is there, but with deep respect. If there is no respect then that is ugly, then the rebellion is not beautiful. Then you are missing something. Rebel, be free, but be respectful because the father, the mother, is the source.

So one has to go away from the parents. Not only away but sometimes, in many ways, against them. But that should not become anger. It should not be ugly, it should remain beautiful, respectful. If you go away, go, but touch the feet of your mother and father. Tell them that you have to go away, cry, but tell them that you are helpless, you *have* to go. The challenge has called you, and you have to go. One cries on leaving home. One goes on looking back again and again, with wistful eyes, nostalgia. The days that have passed were beautiful. But what to do?

If you cling to the home you will remain crippled. You will remain juvenile. You will never become a man in your own right. So what I say to you is to go away with respect. Whenever they need, serve them, be available. But never mistake your mother for your beloved; she is your mother.

The ordinary state of man is that of mechanical functioning: "Homo mechanicus." Only in name are you a man, otherwise just a trained, skillful machine and whatever you do is going to be wrong. And remember, I am saying whatever you do – even your virtues will not be virtues if you are unaware. How can you be virtuous when you are unaware? You will live a respectable life as a saint, but as poor as everybody else: inwardly rotten, inwardly a meaningless existence.

Only one thing is enough; awareness is a master key. It unlocks all the locks of existence. Awareness means you live moment to moment, alert, conscious of yourself and conscious of all that is happening around you, in a moment-to-moment response. You are like a mirror.

The Robot

Why do the Sufis say that man is a machine?

Man *is* a machine, that's why. Man as he is is utterly unconscious. He is nothing but his habits, the sum total of his habits.

Man is a robot. Man is not yet man: unless consciousness enters your being, you will remain a machine.

That's why the Sufis say man is a machine. It is from the Sufis that Gurdjieff introduced the idea to the West that man is a machine. When Gurdjieff said for the first time that man is a machine, it shocked many people. But he was saying the truth.

It is very rare that you are conscious. In your whole seventy years' life, if you live the ordinary so-called life you will not know even seven moments of awareness in your whole life.

And even if you know those seven moments or less, they will be only accidental. For example, you may know a moment of awareness if somebody suddenly comes and puts a revolver on your heart. In that moment, your thinking, your habitual thinking, stops. For a moment you become aware because it is so dangerous; you cannot remain ordinarily asleep.

In some dangerous situations you become aware. Otherwise you remain fast asleep. You are perfectly skillful at doing your things mechanically.

Just stand by the side of the road and watch people, and you will be able to see that they are all walking in their sleep. All are sleepwalkers, somnambulists.

And so are you.

Two bums were arrested and charged with a murder that had been committed in the neighborhood. The jury found them guilty and the judge sentenced them to hang by their necks until dead and God have mercy on their souls.

The two bore up pretty well until the morning of the day set for the execution arrived. As they were being prepared for the gallows, one turned to the other and said, "Dam' me if I ain't about off my nut. I can't get my thoughts together. Why, I don't even know what the day of the week is."

"This is a Monday," said the other bum.

"Monday? My Gawd! What a rotten way to start the week!"

Just watch yourself. Even to the very point of death, people go on repeating old habitual patterns. Man reacts. That's why the Sufis say man is a machine.

Unless you start responding, unless you become responsible... Reaction comes out of the past, response comes out of the present moment. Response is spontaneous, reaction is just old habit.

Just watch yourself. Your woman says something to you: then whatever you say – watch, ponder over it. Is it just a reaction? And you will be surprised: ninety-nine percent of your acts are not acts because they are not responses, they are just mechanical. Just mechanical.

It has been happening again and again: you say the same thing and your woman reacts the same way, and then you react, and it ends in the same thing again and again. You know it, she knows it, everything is predictable.

I have heard...

"Pop," asked a boy of ten, "how do wars get started?"

"Well, son," began Pop, "let's say America quarreled with England..."

"America's not quarreling with England," interrupted Mother.

"Who said she was?" said Pop, visibly irritated. "I was merely giving the boy a hypothetical instance."

"Ridiculous!" snorted Mother. "You'll put all sorts of wrong ideas in his head."

"Ridiculous, nothing!" countered Pop. "If he listens to you, he'll never have any ideas at all in his head!"

Just as the dish-throwing stage approached, the son spoke up again. "Thanks Mom, thanks Pop. I'll never have to ask how wars get started again."

Just watch yourself. The things that you are doing, you have done so many times. The ways you react, you have been reacting always. In the same situation you always do the same thing. You are feeling nervous and you take out your cigarette and you start smoking. It is a reaction; whenever you have felt nervous you have done it.

You are a machine. It is just an inbuilt program in you now: you feel nervous, your hand goes into the pocket, the packet comes out. It is almost like a machine doing things. You take the cigarette out, you put the cigarette in your mouth, you light the cigarette, and this is all going on mechanically. This has been done millions of times and you are doing it again.

And each time you do it, it is strengthened; the machine becomes more mechanical, the machine becomes more skillful. The more you do it, the less awareness is needed to do it.

This is why the Sufis say man functions as a machine. Unless you start destroying these mechanical habits... For example, do something just contrary to what you have always done.

Try it. You come home, you are afraid, you are as late as ever, and the wife will be there ready to quarrel with you. And you are planning how to answer, what to say – that there was too much work in the office, and this and that. And she knows all that you are planning, and she knows what you are going to say if she asks why you are late. And you know if you say that you are late because there was too much work she is not going to believe it either. She has never believed it. She may have already checked; she may have phoned the office, she may have already inquired where you are. But, still, this is just a pattern.

Today go home and behave totally differently. The wife asks you, "Where have you been?" And you say, "I was with a woman making love." And then see what happens. She will be shocked! She will not know what to say, she will not even have any way to find words to express it. For a moment she will be completely lost because no reaction, no old pattern, is applicable.

Or maybe, if she has become too much of a machine, she will say, "I don't believe you!" – just as she has never believed you. "You must be joking!" Every day you come home…

I have heard about a psychoanalyst who was telling his patient, "Today when you go home…" because the patient was complaining again and again. "I am always afraid of going home. My wife looks so miserable, so sad, always in despair, that my heart starts sinking. I want to escape from the home."

The psychologist said, "Maybe you are the cause of it. Do something: today take flowers and ice cream and sweets for the woman, and when she opens the door, hug her, give her a good kiss. And then immediately start helping her: clean the table and the pots and the floor. Do something absolutely new that you have never done before."

The idea was appealing and the man tried it. He went home. The moment the wife opened the door and saw flowers and ice cream and sweets, and this beaming man who had never been laughing hugged her, she could not believe what was happening! She was in an utter shock, she could not believe her eyes: maybe this is somebody else! She had to look again.

And then when he kissed her and immediately just started cleaning the table and went to the sink and started washing the pots, the woman started crying. When he came out he said, "Why are you crying?"

She cried, "Have you gone mad? I always suspected one day or other you would go mad. Now it has happened. Why don't you go and see a psychiatrist?"

Sufis have such devices. They say: Act totally differently, and not only will others be surprised, *you* will be surprised. And just in small things. For example, when you are nervous you walk fast. Don't walk fast, go very slow and see. You will be surprised that it doesn't fit, that your whole mechanical mind immediately says, "What are you doing? You have never done this!" And if you walk slowly you will be surprised: nervousness disappears because you have brought in something new.

These are the methods of *vipassana* and *zazen*. If you go deep into them the fundamentals are the same. When you are doing *vipassana* walking, you have to walk more slowly than you have ever walked before, so slowly that it is absolutely new. The whole feeling is new and the reactive mind cannot function. It cannot function because it has no program for it; it simply stops functioning.

That's why in *vipassana* you feel so silent watching the breath. You have always breathed but you have never watched it; this is something new. When you sit silently and just watch your breath – coming in, going out, coming in, going out – the mind feels puzzled: what are you doing? Because you have never done it. It is so new that the mind cannot supply an immediate reaction to it. Hence it falls silent.

The fundamental is the same. Whether Sufi or Buddhist or Hindu or Mohammedan is not the question. If you go deep into meditation's fundamentals then the essential thing is one: how to deautomatize you.

Gurdjieff used to do very bizarre things to his disciples. Somebody would come who had always been a vegetarian, and he would say, "Eat meat." Now, it is the same fundamental – this man was just a little too much of himself, a little eccentric. He would say, "Eat meat." Now, watch a vegetarian eating meat. The whole body wants to throw it out and he wants to vomit, and the whole mind is puzzled and disturbed and he starts perspiring, because the mind has no way to cope with it.

That's what Gurdjieff wanted to see, how you would react to a new situation. To the man who had never taken any alcohol Gurdjieff would say, "Drink. Drink as much as you can." And to the man who had been drinking alcohol Gurdjieff would say, "Stop for one month. Completely stop."

He wanted to create some situation which is so new for the mind that the mind simply falls silent; it has no answer for it, no ready-made answer for it. The mind functions in a parrot-like way.

That's why Zen masters will hit the disciple sometimes. That is again the same fundamental. Now, when you go to a master you don't expect a buddha to hit you, or do you? When you go to Buddha you go with expectations that he will be compassionate and loving, that he will shower love and put his hand on your head. And this buddha gives you a hit – takes his staff and hits you hard on the head. Now, it is so shocking: a buddha, hitting you? For a moment the mind stops; it has no idea what to do, it does not function.

And that nonfunctioning is the beginning. Sometimes a person has become enlightened just because the master did something absurd.

People have expectations, people live through expectations. They don't know that masters don't fit with any kind of expectations. India was accustomed to Krishna and Rama and people like that. Then came Mahavira, he stood naked. You cannot think of Krishna standing naked; he was always wearing beautiful clothes, as beautiful as possible. He was one of the most beautiful persons ever; he used to wear ornaments made of gold and diamonds. And then suddenly there is Mahavira. What did Mahavira mean by being naked? He shocked the whole country: he helped many people because of that shock.

Each master has to decide how to shock. Now, in India they have not known a man like me for centuries. So whatever I do, whatever I say, is a shock. The whole country goes into shock; a great shiver runs through the spine of the whole country. I really enjoy it because they cannot think...

I am not here to fulfill your expectations. If I fulfill your expectations I will never be able to transform you. I am here to destroy all your expectations, I am here to shock you. And in those shocking experiences your mind will stop. You will not be able to figure it out: and that is the point where something new enters you.

The Sufis say man is a machine because man only reacts according to the programs that have been fed to him. Start behaving responsively, and then you are not a machine. And when you are not a machine, you are a man: then the man is born.

Watch, become alert, observe, and go on dropping all the reactive patterns in you. Each moment try to respond to the reality – not according to the ready-made idea in you but according to the reality as it is there outside. Respond to the reality! Respond with your total consciousness but not with your mind.

And then when you respond spontaneously and you don't react, action is born. Action is beautiful, reaction is ugly. Only a man of awareness acts, the man of unawareness *reacts*. Action liberates. Reaction goes on creating the same chains, goes on making them thicker and harder and stronger.

Live a life of response and not of reaction.

When the cuckoo starts singing, have you ever thought about what the song is for? It is to attract a sexual partner. But nobody condemns the cuckoo as obscene. When the flowers open and send their fragrance, what do you think they are doing? They are advertising that "I have come to flower; now butterflies, bees are invited and welcome." But for what? – because the flower has small seeds which will go with the butterflies, with the bees. Because the same division exists in the whole existence: there are plants which are male, and there are plants which are female. The male plant has to send its seeds to the female plant, its beloved.
Have you seen the dance of a peacock? Do you think he is dancing for you?

The Animal

After eating the fruit of the tree of knowledge, Adam and Eve, for the first time, became aware of their nakedness and felt ashamed. What is the deeper meaning behind this feeling? And, secondly, it has been said that the forbidden fruit of the tree of knowledge is knowledge of sex. What is your view about this?

Nature in itself is innocent, but the moment man becomes aware of it, many problems arise, and what is natural and innocent is interpreted. And when it is interpreted, it is neither innocent nor natural. When humanity becomes aware of it, man begins to interpret it, and the very interpretation begins to produce many concepts – of guilt, of sin, of morality, of immorality.

The story of Adam and Eve says that when the fruit of the tree of knowledge was eaten, for the first time they became aware of their nakedness and felt ashamed. They were naked, but they had never been aware of it. The awareness, the very awareness, creates a gap.

The moment you are aware of something, you begin to judge. You are different from it. For example, Adam was naked. Everyone is born naked like Adam, but children are not aware of their nakedness. They cannot judge it, whether it is good or bad. They are not aware, so they cannot judge. When Adam became aware that he was naked, judgment entered: "Now, is this nakedness good or bad?"

Every animal was naked around him, but no animal was aware of his nakedness. Adam became aware, and with this awareness he became unique. Now to be naked was to be like an animal, and

Adam, of course, would not like to be an animal. No man likes it, although every man is.

When for the first time Darwin said that man is a growth, a growth from certain animals, he was opposed vehemently because man has always been thinking himself a descendant of God, just a little bit lower than the angels. And to conceive of the ape as the father was very difficult, in a way impossible. God was the father and suddenly Darwin changes it: the God is dethroned and apes are enthroned, the ape becomes the father. Even Darwin felt guilty about it; he was a religious man. This was a misfortune that the facts were saying that man has come through animal evolution, he is part of the animal world, he is not something different from animals.

Adam felt ashamed. That shame came because he could now compare himself with the animals. In a way he was different because he was aware. Man clothed himself just to differentiate between the animals and himself. And then we are always ashamed about something which looks like animals. The moment someone is doing something like animals, we say, "What are you doing? Are you an animal?" We can condemn anything if we can prove that "this is just like the animals." We condemn sex because it is animalistic. We can condemn anything if somewhere it can be linked with animals.

With awareness came the condemnation, condemnation of the animal. And this condemnation has produced the whole body of suppression, because man is animal. He can go beyond it – that's another thing – but he belongs to the animals. He can transcend, but he comes from the animals. He is an animal. He may not be one day; he can go beyond, but he cannot deny the animal heritage. It is there.

And once this thought came to the human mind, that we are different from animals, then man began to suppress everything in him that was part of his animal heritage. This suppression has created a bifurcation, so every man is two, double. The real, the basic, remains the animal; and the intellectual, the cerebral, goes on thinking in terms of celestial things, abstract, divine. So only a part of your mind is identified by you as yourself, and the whole is denied.

Even in the body we have divisions. The lower body is something condemned. It is not only lower, it is lower in terms of values also. The upper body is not only upper, it is higher. You will feel guilty about your lower body. And if someone says, "Where are you located?" you will point to your head. That is the locus – the cerebral, the head, the intellect. We identify ourselves with the intellect, not with the body. And if someone presses us more, then we will identify ourselves with the upper body, never with the lower. The lower is something condemned.

Why? The body is one. You cannot divide it, there is no division. The head and feet are one, and your brain and your sex organs are one. They function as a unity. But to deny sex, to condemn sex, we condemn the whole lower body.

This shame came to Adam because for the first time he could feel himself different from other animals. And the most animalistic thing – I use the word *animalistic* in a purely factual way, with no condemnatory tone – the most animalistic thing is bound to appear to be sex, because sex is life and the origin and the source. Adam and Eve became conscious of sex. They tried to hide it – not only outwardly: they tried to hide the very fact even in the inner consciousness. That created the division between the conscious and the unconscious mind.

The mind is also one, just like the body is one. But if you condemn something, then that condemned part will become unconscious. You condemn it so much that you yourself become afraid of knowing it, that it exists somewhere within you. You create a barrier, you create a wall, and throw everything that is condemned by you beyond the wall, then you can forget it. It remains there, it goes on working from there, it remains your master, yet you can deceive yourself that now it is no more.

That condemned part of our being becomes the unconscious. That's why we never think that our unconscious is ours. You dream in the night: you dream a very sexual dream, or a violent dream, and you murder someone – you murder your wife. In the morning you feel no guilt; you say it was just a dream. It is not just a dream. Nothing is just something. It was your dream, but it belongs to your unconscious. And in the morning you identify yourself with the conscious, so you say, "It is just a dream. It doesn't belong to me. It just happened. It is irrelevant, accidental." You never feel associated with it. But it was your dream and you created it. It was your mind and it was you who did the act. Even in the dream it was you who murdered, who killed or who raped.

Because of this condemnatory phenomenon of consciousness,

Adam and Eve became afraid, ashamed of their nakedness. They tried to hide their bodies – not only their bodies, but later on their minds also. So we are also doing the same thing. What is good, what is taken as good by our society, you put it in your conscious; what is bad, what is condemned by our society as bad, you throw into the unconscious. It becomes a rubbish bag. You go on throwing things into it – it remains there. Deep down in your roots it goes on working. It affects you every moment. Your conscious mind is just impotent against your unconscious, because your conscious mind is just a byproduct of the society and your unconscious is natural, biological. It has the energy, the force. So you can go on thinking good things, but you will go on doing bad things.

Saint Augustine is reported to have said, "My God, this is the only problem for me: whatever I think is worth doing I never do, and whatever I know is not to be done I do always." This is not a problem only for Augustine – it is for everyone who is divided between conscious and unconscious.

With the feeling of shame, Adam was divided into two. He became ashamed of himself, and that part he became ashamed of was cut loose from his conscious mind. Since then man has lived a bifurcated, fragmented life.

And why did he become ashamed? There was no one, no preacher, no religious church, to tell him to be ashamed. The moment you become aware, the ego enters. You become an observer. Without awareness you are just a part, a part of a great life; you are not different and separate. If a wave in the ocean can become aware, the wave will create an ego different from the ocean that very moment. If the wave becomes aware that "I am," then the wave can never think itself one with the ocean, one with other waves. It becomes different, separate; ego is created. Knowledge creates the ego.

Children are without egos because they are without knowledge. They are ignorant, and ego cannot come up in ignorance. The more you grow, the more you grow toward ego. Old men have very strengthened, deep-rooted egos. It is natural. Their egos have existed for seventy or eighty years. They have a long history.

If you go back in memory and remember your childhood, you may be surprised to know why you cannot remember, you cannot regress beyond your fourth or third year. You can remember, ordinarily we remember, facts which belong to our fifth year or fourth year, at the most the third year, but the first three years are just vacant. They were there and many things happened, but why can we not remember? Because the ego was not there it is difficult to remember – because, in a way, you were not, so how can you remember? If you were there you would remember, but you were not. You cannot remember.

Memory exists only after the ego has come into existence, because the memory needs a center to hang on. If you are not, where will the memory hang? Three years is a big thing, and for a child every moment is an event. Everything is something phenomenal, nothing is ordinary. So, really, he should remember more of the first years, the first days of life, because everything was colorful, everything was unique. Whatever happened was new. But there is no memory of it. Why? The ego was not there and memory needs an ego to hang on.

The moment the child begins to feel himself as separate from others, he will begin to feel shame. He will begin to feel the same shame that came to Adam. He found himself naked – naked like the animals, naked like everyone else. You must be different and unique, you must not be like others, only then can you grow in ego.

The first act was to hide the nakedness: he became suddenly different. He was not an animal. Man is born. With Adam, and with Adam's shame, with Adam's feeling of shame, man is born. A child is not a man. He becomes a man only when he begins to feel himself separate, different from others, then he becomes an ego.

So, really, it is not religion which gives you the feeling of guilt, it is your ego. Religion exploits it; that's another matter. Every father exploits it; that is another matter. Every father is saying to his son, "What are you doing, behaving like an animal? Don't laugh, don't cry! Don't do this, don't do that; don't do this before others! What are you doing? – behaving like an animal!" And the child feels that if he is an animal, his ego is hurt. To fulfill his ego he follows, he falls in line.

To be animal is very blissful, because there is a freedom, a deep freedom, to move, to do. But it hurts the ego, so one has to choose. If you choose freedom, then you will be like the animals, condemned. In this world and in the other world to come, you will be condemned. You will be thrown into hell. "Be a man. Don't be like an animal."

The ego is fed. One begins to live around the ego. Then one begins to act according to what is ego-fulfilling. But you cannot deny nature absolutely. It goes on affecting you. Then one begins to live two lives: one, the pre-Adam life; the other, the after-Adam life. So one begins to live two lives, one begins to live a double-bind existence. Then a face is created to show to the society. One is a private face and one a public face. But you are your private face. And everyone is Adam, naked, animal-like, but you cannot show it to the public. To the public you show the after-Adam face: everything clean, everything fitted to the social norm, everything to show for the others; not the real but the desired, not that which is but that which should be.

So everyone has to go continuously from one face to another. From private to public you are changing every moment. This is a great strain. This dissipates much energy. But what am I saying and what do I mean? I don't say be like the animals; you cannot be now. The forbidden fruit cannot be returned. You have eaten it; it has become your blood and bones. There is no way of throwing it. There is no way to return it and go to God the Father and say, "I return this – this forbidden fruit of knowledge. Forgive me." There is no way. There is no way to go back. Now it is our blood.

We cannot go back, we can only go forward. There is no going back. We cannot go below knowledge, we can only go beyond knowledge. Only a different innocence is possible – the innocence of total awareness.

There are two types of innocence. One, below knowledge: the childlike, the pre Adam-like, animal-like, below knowledge. You are not, the ego is not, the troublemaker is not. You exist as part of the cosmic whole. You don't know that you are part. You don't know that there is a cosmic whole. You know nothing. You exist without knowing. Of course there is no suffering, because suffering is impossible without knowledge. One has to be aware of suffering to suffer it. How can you suffer if you are not aware?

You are being operated upon, a surgeon is operating on you. You suffer if you are conscious. If you are unconscious, there is no suffering. The leg is cut off completely, thrown; there is no suffering because suffering is nowhere recorded, nowhere known, you are unconscious. You cannot suffer in unconsciousness. You can suffer only when you are conscious. The more conscious, the more you will suffer. That's why the more man grows in knowledge, the more he suffers.

Primitive people cannot suffer so much as you can suffer, not because they are better but because they are ignorant. Villagers, even today, villagers who are not yet part of the modern world, live in a more innocent way. They don't suffer so much. Because of this, many fallacies have come to the thinkers, to philosophers. For example, Rousseau or Tolstoy or Gandhi: they think because villagers are more blissful it would be good if the whole world became primitive again, went back to the jungle, back to the forest, back to nature. But they are wrong because the man who has lived in a civilized city will suffer in a village. No villager has suffered that way.

So Rousseau goes on talking about "back to nature" and continues to live in Paris. He himself will never go to the village. He talks about the poetry of village life, of the beauty, of the innocence, but he himself will never go. And if he goes, he will know that he will suffer as no villager has suffered, because once consciousness is attained you cannot throw it – because it is you. It is not something that you can throw. It is you – how can you throw yourself? Consciousness is you.

Adam suffered shame; he felt his nakedness. Ego is the reason. Adam attained a center, though false, but still a center. Now Adam was different from the whole cosmos. The trees were there, the stars were there, everything was there, but Adam was now an island, separate. Now his life was his life, not part of the cosmic whole. And the moment your life is your life, struggle enters. You have to fight inch by inch to exist, to survive.

Animals are not in a struggle. Even if they appear to us, to a Darwin, to be in a struggle, they are not in a struggle. They appear to Darwin to be in a struggle because we go on projecting our own ideas. They cannot be in a struggle. They appear to us to be in a struggle because for us everything is a struggle. With the ego everything is a struggle. They seem to be fighting to be. They are not fighting to be: they are just flowing in the cosmic unity. Even if they are doing something, there is no doer behind it. It is a natural phenomenon.

A lion killing some victim for his food: there is no doer, there is no violence. It is a simple phenomenon: just hunger after food. There is no hungry one: simple hunger, a mechanism finding the food, no violence. Only man can be violent because only man can be a doer. You can kill without hunger. A lion can never kill without hunger because hunger kills in a lion, not the lion. A lion can never kill in play. There is nothing like hunting for a lion, it exists only for man. You can kill in play, just for fun. If a lion is satisfied, there is no violence, no play, no game, nothing. It is a hunger phenomenon. The doer is not there.

Nature exists as a deep cosmic flow. In this flow Adam becomes aware of himself, and he becomes aware because he has eaten the forbidden fruit of knowledge. Knowledge was forbidden: "Don't eat the fruit of the tree of knowledge" was the commandment. He disobeyed it, he couldn't go back. And the Bible says every man will suffer for Adam's rebelliousness because in a way every man is an Adam again.

You cannot suffer for it – how can you suffer for something someone else did somewhere? But it is a continuous history repeated every day. Every child has to pass from the Garden of Eden to the expulsion. Every child is born as Adam and then he is expelled. That's why there is so much nostalgia in poets, in painters, in literary persons, in all those who can manipulate to express. There is a nostalgia always. The golden age was childhood.

Everyone thinks that childhood was something golden, utopian, and everyone longs to go back to it. Even an old man, just on the deathbed, thinks with nostalgia of childhood: of the beauty, of the happiness, of the bliss, of the flowers, of the butterflies, of the dreams, of fairies. Everyone in his childhood is in a wonderland, not only Alice, everyone. This shadow follows....

Why is childhood so beautiful, so blissful? Because you were still a part of the cosmic flow, with no responsibility, with absolute freedom, with no conscience, with no burden. You existed as if it was not something to be done by you. It was there, taken for granted. And then comes the ego, and then comes the conflict, and the struggle. Then everything becomes a responsibility, and every moment is a bondage, no freedom.

Psychologists say that religions only reflect this nostalgia to be again in childhood. And they go even further: they say ultimately everyone longs to be again in the mother's womb, because then you were really part of the cosmos. The cosmos was even feeding you. Even to breathe was not for you to do; the mother was breathing for you. You were not aware of the mother, you were not aware of yourself. You were there with no awareness.

The womb is the Garden of Eden. So every man is born as an Adam, and everyone has to eat the forbidden fruit of knowledge, because the moment you grow, you grow in knowledge. That is inevitable. So it is not that Adam rebelled. Rebellion is part of growth. He couldn't do otherwise: he had to. Every child has to rebel, has to disobey. Life demands it. He has to go further away from the mother, from the father. He will long for it again; again and again he will desire and dream, but still he will go further away. This is an inevitable process.

It is asked: "What is the deeper meaning behind this feeling?" This is the meaning: knowledge gives you ego, and ego gives you comparison, judgment, individuality. You cannot think of yourself as an animal, so man has done everything to hide the fact that he is an animal. He has done everything! We are doing things every day to hide the fact that we are animals. But we are. And by hiding the fact, the fact is not destroyed; rather, it becomes a perverted fact.

So whenever that hidden perversion erupts, man proves to be more animalistic than any animal. If you are violent, no animal can compete with you. How? No animal has known anything like Hiroshima, Vietnam. Only man can create a Hiroshima. There is no comparison. All the animals in all the history are just playing with dolls in comparison to Hiroshima. Their violence is nothing. This is accumulated violence – hidden, accumulated. We go on hiding and then we are accumulating. And the more we accumulate, the more ashamed we feel, because we know what is hidden inside. You cannot escape it.

A certain psychologist was experimenting with hidden facts, which, howsoever you try, you cannot hide. For example, if someone says that he is not attracted to women, he can practice it. He can practice it and he can convince himself and others also that he is not attracted. But Adam is bound to be attracted to Eve, Eve is bound to be attracted to Adam. That is part of their nature, unless one goes beyond, unless one becomes a buddha.

But then Buddha never says, "I am not attracted to women," because even to say that, you have to think in terms of attraction and repulsion. He will not say, "I am repelled by women," because you cannot be repelled by anything unless you are attracted. If you ask him he will simply say, "Men and women, both have become irrelevant to me. I am neither. If I am man, then woman will be there hidden somewhere. If I am woman, then man will be there hidden somewhere."

One psychologist just recently experimented with a man who said, "I am not attracted to women." And he was not, as far as outward things go. He was never seen to be attracted to anyone. Then this psychologist showed him some pictures, ten pictures, of different things, only one picture of a naked woman.

The psychologist was not seeing what picture the man was seeing. He was just looking in the man's eyes; the back of the picture was in front of the psychologist. He would show a picture to the man and just look in his eyes. And he said, "If you are not attracted… I will tell you when you are seeing the naked woman just by seeing your eyes. I am not seeing the pictures."

The pictures were shown, and with that very picture the psychologist said, "Now you are seeing the naked woman," because the moment a naked woman is there, the eyes extend. And that is involuntary; you cannot control it. You cannot do anything. It is a reflex action. Eyes are made that way biologically. The man says that "I am not attracted," but this is only his conscious mind. The unconscious is attracted all the same.

And when you hide certain facts and they go on manipulating you, you become more and more ashamed. The higher a civilization, the higher its culture, the more ashamed the human being will be – the more ashamed. Really, the more ashamed you are about sex, the more civilized you are. But then civilized man is bound to be insane, schizophrenic, divided. This division starts with Adam.

"And, secondly, it has been said that the forbidden fruit of the tree of knowledge is knowledge of sex. What is your view about this?" Of course it is. But not only that: sex is the first knowledge and sex is also the last knowledge. When you enter humanity, the first thing you begin to feel and be aware of is sex. And the last thing, when you go beyond humanity, is again sex – the last thing and the first. Because sex is the most foundational, it is bound to be the first. It is the alpha and the omega.

A child is just a child unless he becomes sexually mature. The moment he becomes sexually mature, he is a man. With sexual maturity, the whole world becomes different. It is not the same world because your approach, your outlook, your way of seeing things, changes. When you begin to be aware of the woman, you begin to be a man.

Really, in old biblical texts, "knowledge" is used in the Hebrew language with a sexual meaning. For example, in such sentences: "He didn't know his wife for two years," or, "She didn't know her husband for two years," it means there was no sexual relationship for two years. "He knew his wife for the first time on that day": it means there was a sexual relationship for the first time. Knowledge in Hebrew is used for sexual knowledge, so it is right that Adam became aware of sex then.

Sex is most foundational. Without sex there is no life. Life exists because of sex and life disappears with sex. That's why Buddha and Mahavira say unless you go beyond sex you will be born again and again. You cannot go beyond life because with a sexual desire inside, you will be born again. So sex is not only giving birth to someone else; ultimately, it is giving birth to yourself also. It works in a double way. You reproduce someone through sex, but that is not so important. Because of your sexual desire, you are reborn; you reproduce yourself again and again.

Adam became aware of his sex; that was the first awareness. But with sex it is only a beginning. Then everything else will follow.

Really, psychologists say that every curiosity is sexual in a way. So if a person is born impotent, he will not be curious about anything – not even about truth, because curiosity of any type is basically sexual. To discover something hidden, to know something which is not known, to know the unknown, is sexual. Children will play with each other to find out the hidden parts of the body. That is the beginning of curiosity and the beginning of all science: to find out that which is hidden, that which is not known.

So really it happens that the more sexual a person is, the more inventive he can be. The more sexual a person is, the more intelligent. With less sex energy, less intelligence exists; with more sexual energy, more intelligence, because sex is a deep search to uncover, not only bodies, not only the opposite sex body, but everything that is hidden.

So if a society is very sex-condemnatory, it can never be scientific because then you condemn curiosity. The East could not be scientific because of so much antagonism toward sex. And the West also could not be scientific as long as Christianity retained its hold. It was only when the Vatican disappeared, when Rome was not significant at all, only within these three hundred years when the palace of Christianity came down and disappeared, that the West could be scientific. The release of sexual energy also became a release into research. A sexually free society will be scientific, and a sexually prohibitive society will be nonscientific.

With sex everything begins to be alive. If your child, when he attains maturity, sexual maturity, begins to behave rebelliously, forgive him. It is but natural. With a new energy coming into his veins, with new life running, he is bound to be rebellious. That rebellion is just part of it. He is also bound to be inventive. He will invent new things, new ways, new styles, new manners of life, new societies. He will dream new dreams, he will think about new utopias. If you condemn sex, then there is no rebellion of youth. All over the world, the rebellion of youth is part of a sexual freedom.

In the old cultures there was no rebellion because sex was so much condemned, the energy was so much suppressed. With that energy suppressed, every rebellion is suppressed. If you give freedom to sex energy, every rebellion will be there, every type of rebellion will be there.

Knowledge in itself has a sexual dimension, so it is right in a way that Adam became aware of sex, the dimension of sex. But with that dimension of sex he became aware of many other things also. This whole expansion of knowledge, this explosion of knowledge, this probing into the unknown, this going to the moon and to other planets, it is a sexual thirst. And the West will go further and further into knowledge because now the energy is released, and now the energy will take new shapes, new adventures.

With sex and the awareness of sex, Adam started on a long journey. We are on it, everyone is on it, because sex is not just a part of your body – it is you. You are born of sex and you will die of sex, exhausted. Your birth is the birth of sex, and your death is the death of sex. So the moment you feel that the sexual energy is waning, know that death is coming near.

Thirty-five is the peak age. Sex energy is at the peak and then everything declines, then one begins to be old, on the downward path. Seventy will be the death age. If fifty can be the peak of sexual energy, then a hundred will be the death age. The West will soon attain a hundred years as a normal, average age, because now a fifty-year-old man is behaving like a boy. It is good, it shows an alive society. It shows that now life will be lengthened.

If a hundred-year-old man can behave like a playboy, then life will be lengthened to two hundred years – because sex is the energy. Because of sex you are young and because of sex you will be old. Because of sex you are born and because of sex you will die. And not only that: Buddha and Mahavira and Krishna say that because of sexual desire you will be born again. Not only is this body run by sex, but all your bodies in continuity are run by sexual desire.

Of course, when Adam became conscious for the first time, he became conscious of sex. That is the most foundational fact. But this was misinterpreted by Christianity and then much nonsense followed. It was said: Because Adam became aware of his sex and felt ashamed, sex is bad and a sin, original sin. It is not. It is original life. He became ashamed, not because sex is bad: he became ashamed because he saw that sex is an animal affair and "I am not an animal." So sex has to be fought, cut out, and thrown. Somehow one has to become without sex. This is a misinterpretation, the Christian interpretation of the parable: "So fight against sex." Religion became just a fight against sex. And if religion is a fight against sex, then religion is a fight against life.

To me, religion is not a fight against sex. Rather, it is an effort to go beyond, not against. If you are against, you will remain on the same level with sex. Then you can never go beyond. So Christian mystics and saints are fighting to their deathbed against sex. And the temptation comes, and every moment they are tempted. There is no one to tempt them...their own suppression. In their own suppression is the creation of their temptation. They live in a very tortured world of inner mind where they are constantly fighting with themselves.

Religion is to go beyond, not against. And if you want to go beyond, you have to step, to use sex energy to transcend it. You have to move with it, not fight with it. You have to know it more. To be ignorant now is impossible – you have to know it more. Knowledge is freedom. If you know it more and more and more, and a moment comes when you are totally aware, sex disappears. In that total awareness, the energy is transformed, mutated. You now have a different dimension of the same energy.

Sex is horizontal. When you are totally aware, sex becomes vertical. And that vertical movement of sex is kundalini. If sex moves horizontally, then you go on reproducing others and reproducing yourself. If the energy begins to move upward, vertically, you just go out – out of the wheel of existence, as the Buddhists say, out of the wheel of life. It is a new birth: not in a new body, but in a new dimension of existence. This Buddhists have called nirvana, or *moksha*, or whatever you like to call it you can call it. Names don't mean much.

So there are two ways. Adam becomes aware of his sex. He can suppress it; then he will move horizontally, fighting with it, in a constant anguish, always knowing the animal is hidden inside and always pretending that it is not there. This is the anguish. And one can move horizontally for lives together, reaching nowhere, because it is a repetitive circle. That's why we call it a wheel, a repetitive circle.

You can jump out of the wheel. That jump will not be through suppression; it will be through more knowledge. So I will say: you have eaten the fruit of the forbidden tree – now eat the whole tree! That is the only way. Now eat the whole tree. Don't leave even a single leaf. Let there be no tree. Eat it totally. Only then will you be freed of knowledge, never before.

And with that, when I say eat the whole tree I mean now, when you have become aware, be aware totally. Fragmentary awareness is the problem. Either be totally ignorant or be totally aware. Totality is bliss. Be totally ignorant – you are in bliss. You will not be aware of it, but you will be in bliss. Just as we are when we are deep asleep, not even dreaming, simply asleep, with no movement of the mind – you are in bliss, but you cannot feel it. You can say in the morning that the night's sleep was very blissful, but it was not felt when the sleep was there. It is felt only when you have come out of it. When knowledge enters, awareness comes, you can say the night was very blissful.

Either be totally ignorant, which is impossible, or be totally knowing, which is possible. With totality there is bliss. Totality is bliss. So eat the tree, root and all, and be aware. This is what is meant by an awakened man, a buddha, an enlightened man: he has eaten the whole tree. Now nothing is left to be aware. A simple awareness exists.

This simple awareness is a re-entry into Eden. You cannot find the old gate again; it is missed forever. You can find a new gate; you can enter again. And, really, whatever the Devil promised to Adam will be fulfilled: you will be like gods. He was right in a way. If you eat the fruit of knowledge, you will be like gods.

We cannot conceive this in this state of mind, because we are just in a hell; because of this Devil's temptation, we are in a hell. We are as if suspended in between two things, always divided, in agony, in anguish. It seems that the Devil deceived Adam, deceived us. This is not the whole thing; the story is incomplete. You can complete it, and only then can you judge whether whatever the Devil said was right or not. Eat the whole tree and you will be like gods.

A person who has become totally aware is divine, he is not human. Humanity is a sort of disease. I say dis-ease, a continuous dis-ease. Either be like animals, you are healthy; or be like gods, you are healthy – healthy because whole, a wholeness.

The English word *holy* is good. It doesn't mean only pure; really it means to be whole. And unless you are whole you cannot be holy. Be whole. And there are only two types of wholeness: one, the animal type; the other, the godly type.

A married couple took their little boy to the circus. During the gorilla act the husband had to go to the bathroom, and while he was gone, the little boy nudged his mother and said, "What is that long thing hanging down between the gorilla's legs?"

His mother was very embarrassed and said quickly, "Oh, that's nothing, dear."

When the husband returned, the wife went off to buy some popcorn, and while she was gone, the little boy nudged his father and said, "Daddy, what is that big thing hanging down between the gorilla's legs?"

The father smiled and said, "That, son, is his penis."

The little boy looked puzzled for a moment and then said, "Then why did mummy just say it was nothing?"

"Son," said his father proudly, "I have spoiled that woman."

Sex is a subtle subject, delicate, because centuries of exploitation, corruption, centuries of perverted ideas, conditioning, are associated with the word sex. *The word is very loaded. It is one of the most loaded words in existence. You say "God" – it seems empty. You say "sex" – it seems too loaded. A thousand and one things arise in the mind: fear, perversion, attraction, a tremendous desire, and a tremendous anti-desire also. They all arise together.*

The Sex Maniac

Sex – the very word creates confusion, a chaos. It is as if somebody has thrown a rock in a silent pool; millions of ripples arise – just the word *sex*! Humanity has lived under very wrong ideas.

Have you watched that at a certain age, sex becomes important? Not that you make it important. It is not something that you make happen; it happens. At the age of fourteen, somewhere near there, suddenly the energy is flooded with sex. It happens as if the floodgates have been opened in you. Subtle sources of energy which were not yet open have become open, and your whole energy becomes sexual, colored with sex. You think sex, you sing sex, you walk sex – everything becomes sexual. Every act is colored. This happens; you have not done anything about it. It is natural. Transcendence is also natural. If sex is lived totally, with no condemnation, with no idea of getting rid of it, then at the age of forty-two – just as at the age of fourteen sex gets opened and the whole energy becomes sexual, at the age of forty-two or near about those flood-gates close again. And that too is as natural as sex becoming alive; it starts disappearing.

Sex is transcended not by any effort on your part. If you make any effort that will be repressive, because it has nothing to do with you. It is inbuilt in your body, in your biology. You are born as sexual beings; nothing is wrong in it. That is the only way to be born. To be human is to be sexual. When you were conceived, your mother and your father were not praying, they were not listening to a priest's sermon. They were not in church, they were making love. Even to think that your mother and father were making love when you were conceived seems to be difficult. They were making love;

their sexual energies were meeting and merging into each other. Then you were conceived; in a deep sexual act you were conceived. The first cell was a sex cell, and then out of that cell other cells have arisen. But each cell remains sexual, basically. Your whole body is sexual, made of sex cells. Now they are millions.

Remember: you exist as a sexual being. Once you accept it, the conflict that has been created down through the centuries dissolves. Once you accept it deeply, with no ideas in between, when sex is thought of as simply natural, you live it. You don't ask me how to transcend eating, you don't ask me how to transcend breathing – because no religion has taught you to transcend breathing, that's why. Otherwise, you would be asking, "How to transcend breathing?" You breathe! You are a breathing animal; you are a sexual animal also. But there is a difference. Fourteen years of your life, in the beginning, are almost nonsexual, or at the most, just rudimentary sexual play which is not really sexual – just preparing, rehearsing, that's all. At the age of fourteen, suddenly the energy is ripe.

Watch... A child is born – immediately, within three seconds the child has to breathe, otherwise he will die. Then breathing is to remain the whole of his life, because it has come at the first step of life. It cannot be transcended. Maybe before you die then, just three seconds before, it will stop, but not before it. Always remember: both ends of life, the beginning and end, are exactly similar, symmetrical. The child is born, he starts breathing in three seconds. When the child is old and dying, the moment he stops breathing, within three seconds he will be dead.

Sex enters at a very late stage: for fourteen years the child has lived without sex. And if the society is not too repressed and hence obsessed with sex, a child can live completely oblivious to the fact that sex, or that anything like sex, exists. The child can remain absolutely innocent. That innocence is also not possible because people are so repressed. When repression happens, then side by side, obsession also happens.

So priests go on repressing; and there are anti-priests, the Hugh Hefners and others – they go on creating more and more pornography. So on one side there are priests who go on repressing, and then there are others, anti-priests, who go on making sexuality more and more glamorous. They both exist together – aspects of the same coin. When churches disappear, only then *Playboy* magazines will disappear, not before it. They are partners in the business. They look enemies, but don't be deceived by that. They talk against each other, but that's how things work.

I have heard about two men who were out of business, had gone broke, so they decided for a business, a very simple business. They started journeying, touring from one town to another town. First one would enter, and in the night he would throw coal tar on people's windows and doors. After two or three days the other would come to clean. He would advise that he could clean any coal tar, or anything that had gone wrong, and he would clean the windows. In that time the other would be doing half of the business in another town. This way, they started earning much money.

This is what is happening between the church and Hugh Hefners and people who are continuously creating pornography.

I have heard...

Pretty Miss Keneen sat in the confessional. "Father," she said, "I want to confess that I let my boyfriend kiss me."

"Is that all you did?" asked the priest, very interested.

"Well, no. I let him put his hand on my leg too."

"And then what?"

"And then I let him pull down my panties."

"And then, and then...?"

"And then me mother walked into the room."

"Oh shit," sighed the priest.

It is together; they are partners in a conspiracy. Whenever you are too repressed, you start finding a perverse interest. A perverted interest is the problem, not sex. Now this priest is neurotic. Sex is not the problem, but this man is in trouble.

Sisters Margaret Alice and Francis Catherine were out walking along a side street. Suddenly they were grabbed by two men, dragged into a dark alley, and raped.

"Father, forgive them," said Sister Margaret Alice, "for they know not what they do."

"Shut up!" cried Sister Catherine, "This one does."

This is bound to be so. So never carry a single idea against sex in your mind, otherwise you will never be able to transcend it. People who transcend sex are people who accept it very naturally. It is difficult, I know, because you are born in a society which is neurotic about sex. Either this way or that, but it is neurotic all the same. It is very difficult to get out of this neurosis, but if you are a little alert, you can get out of it. So the real thing is not how to transcend sex, but how to transcend this perverted ideology of the society: this fear of sex, this repression of sex, this obsession with sex.

Sex is beautiful. Sex in itself is a natural rhythmic phenomenon. It happens when the child is ready to be conceived, and it is good that it happens – otherwise life would not exist. Life exists through sex; sex is its medium. If you understand life, if you love life, you will know sex is sacred, holy. Then you live it, then you delight in it; and as naturally as it has come it goes, on its own accord. By the age of forty-two, or somewhere near there, sex starts disappearing as naturally as it had come into being. But it doesn't happen that way.

You will be surprised when I say near about forty-two. You know people who are seventy, eighty, and yet they have not gone beyond. You know "dirty old people." They are victims of the society. Because they could not be natural, it is a hangover – because they repressed when they should have enjoyed and delighted. In those moments of delight they were not totally in it. They were not orgasmic, they were halfhearted. So whenever you are halfhearted in anything, it lingers longer.

This is my understanding: that people, if they have lived rightly, lovingly, naturally, by the forty-second year start transcending sex. If they have not lived naturally and they have been fighting with sex, then forty-two becomes their most dangerous time – because by the time they are forty-two their energies are declining. When you are young you can repress something because you are very energetic. Look at the irony of the fact: a young man can repress sexuality very easily because he has energy to repress it. He can just put it down and sit upon it. When the energies are going, declining, then sex will assert itself and you will not be able to control it.

I have heard an anecdote:

Stein, aged sixty-five, visited the office of his son, Dr. Stein, and asked for something that would increase his sexual potential. The M.D. gave his father a shot, and then refused to accept a fee.

Nevertheless, Stein insisted on giving him ten dollars.

A week later Stein was back for another injection, and this time handed his son twenty dollars. "But Pop, shots are only ten dollars."

"Take it!" said Stein, "The extra ten is from Momma."

That will continue... So before you become a poppa or a momma, please be finished with it. Don't wait for old age because then things go ugly. Then everything goes out of season.

Why am I so fascinated by pornography?

Must be your religious upbringing, Sunday school; otherwise, there is no need to be interested in pornography. When you are against the real, you start imagining. The day religious upbringing disappears from the earth, pornography will die. It cannot die before it. This looks very paradoxical. Magazines like *Playboy* exist only with the support of the Vatican. Without the Pope there will be no *Playboy* magazine; it cannot exist. It will not have any reason to exist. The priest is behind it.

Why should you be interested in pornography when alive people are here? And it is so beautiful to look at alive people. You don't become interested in a picture of a naked tree, do you? Because all trees are naked! Just do one thing: cover all the trees, and sooner or later you will find magazines circulating underground – naked trees! And people will be reading them, putting them inside their Bibles and looking at them and enjoying. Try it and you will see.

Pornography can disappear only when people accept their nudity naturally. You don't want to see cats and dogs and lions and tigers naked in pictures – they *are* naked! In fact, when a dog passes you, you don't even recognize the fact; you don't take note of it that he is naked. There are a few ladies in England, I have heard, who cover their dogs with clothes. They are afraid – the nudity of the dog may disturb some religious, spiritual soul. I have heard, Bertrand Russell has written in his autobiography that in his childhood days those were the days, Victorian days – that even the legs of the chairs were covered, because they are *legs*.

Let man be natural and pornography disappears. Let people be nude...not that they have to sit nude in their offices; there is no need to go that far. But on the beaches, on the rivers, or when they are at ease, relaxing in their homes, resting under the sun in their gardens, they should be nude! Let children play around nude, around [their] nude mother and father. Pornography will disappear! Who will look at the *Playboy* magazine? for what? Something is being deprived, some natural curiosity is being deprived, hence pornography.

Get rid of the priest within you, say goodbye. And then suddenly you will see that pornography has disappeared. Kill the priest in your unconscious, and you will see a great change happening in your being. You will be more together.

Part 2

ADAM AND EVE

Man has to learn how to love. Man has to learn how to let the heart be the master and the mind be just an obedient servant. Man has to learn these things. The woman brings these things with her, but we condemn all these qualities as weaknesses.

Women are women and men are men; there is no question of comparison. Equality is out of the question. They are not unequal and neither can they be equal. They are unique. Man is not in a better position than woman as far as religious experience is concerned. But he has one quality, and that is of the warrior. Once he gets a challenge, then he can grow any kind of qualities. He can even grow the feminine qualities better than any woman can; his fighting spirit balances things. Women have these qualities inborn. Man needs only to be provoked, given a challenge: these qualities have not been given to you – you have to earn them. And if men and women both can live these qualities, the day is not far away when we can transform this world into a paradise.

I would like the whole world to be full of feminine qualities. Only then can wars disappear. Only then can marriage disappear. Only then can nations disappear. Only then can we have one world: a loving, a peaceful, a silent and beautiful world.

The world suffers too much from conflict because of male energy and the domination by it. A balance is needed. I am not saying that the male energy is not needed at all; it is needed, but in proportion. Right now, ninety-nine percent is male energy and the woman exists only on the margin. She is not the main current of life, hence there is strife, struggle, fight, war. That energy has brought humanity to the brink of total suicide. It can happen any day, unless the feminine energy is released to balance it. That is the only hope.

Macho Man

> A woman friend of mine often uses the words "male ego" about me, which I feel is not true. From the very beginning I have been open and vulnerable to feminine energy. Moreover, I have felt that when she uses this word there is some kind of hatred toward men. Can you explain what the "male ego" is, and what it means when a woman uses this expression about a man?

The ego is simply the ego, it is neither male nor female.

But man has been very inhuman toward women for centuries, continuously. And the strange thing is that the man has been so cruel and inhuman toward women because he feels a deep inferiority complex in comparison to them. The greatest problem has been that the woman is capable of becoming a mother; she is capable of giving birth to life and man is not. That was the beginning of the feeling of inferiority – that nature depends on woman, not on man.

Moreover, he has found that she is in many ways stronger than him. Women are more patient, more tolerant than men. Men are very impatient and very intolerant. Women are less violent than men. Women don't commit murders; it is the man who commits murders, who wages crusades, who is always getting ready for war, who invents all kinds of deadly weapons – atomic bombs, nuclear weapons. The woman is completely out of this whole game of death. Hence it was no coincidence that man started feeling somehow inferior. And nobody wants to be inferior; the only way was to force the woman to become inferior in artificial ways. For example, not to allow her education, not to allow her economic freedom, not to allow her to move out of the house, but confine her to an imprisonment. It seems almost unbelievable what man has done to woman just to get rid of his inferiority. He has made the woman artificially inferior.

It is not only a question for you. When your woman is telling you that you have a male ego she is simply representing all women, and you are nothing but a representative of all men. Your forefathers have done so much harm that there is no way to come to a balance. So when your woman says that this is male ego, try to understand. Perhaps she is right. Most probably she is right – because the male has accepted himself as superior for so long that he does not feel that it is his ego. It is the woman who feels it.

Don't deny her feeling. Be grateful to her, and ask her where she feels the ego so that you can drop it. Take her help.

You are simply denying it; you don't feel that you have any male ego. But it is simply a traditional heritage. Every small boy has a male ego. Just a small boy, if he starts crying you immediately say, “Why are you crying like a girl? A girl is allowed to cry because she is subhuman. You are going to be a big male chauvinist; you are not supposed to cry or weep.” And small boys start stopping their tears. It is very rare to find men who are as ready to cry and allow tears to flow as women are.

Listen to the woman. You have suppressed the woman and oppressed the woman so much, it is time that she should be listened to and things should be corrected. At least in your personal life do as much as you can to allow the woman as much freedom as possible – the same freedom that you allow yourself. Help her to stand up so that she can blossom again.

We will have a more beautiful world if all women – and women are half of the world – are allowed to grow their talents, their genius. It is not a question at all... Nobody is higher, nobody is lower. Women are women, men are men; they have differences, but differences don't make anybody higher or lower. Their differences create their attraction. Just think of a world where there are only men. It will be so ugly. Life is rich because there are differences, different attitudes, different opinions. Nobody is superior, nobody is inferior. People are simply different.

Accept this, and help your woman to be free from ten thousand years of repression. Be a friend to her. Much harm has been done; she has been wounded so much that if you can do some healing with your love you will be contributing to the whole world, to the whole world consciousness.

Don't feel bad if your woman says, “This is male ego.” It is there in a subtle form, unrecognizeable because it has been there for so long; you have forgotten that this is ego. Take her help so that you can recognize it and destroy it.

You fall in love with a woman because she is new: the physiology, the proportions of her body, the face, the eyes, the eyebrows, the color of her hair, the way she walks, the way she turns, the way she says hello, the way she looks. Everything is new, the whole territory unknown: you would like to investigate this territory. It is inviting, it is very inviting; you are caught, hypnotized.
But once the woman is conquered; now how can that old interest remain? At the most one can pretend, but the old interest cannot remain. Now there are other women who are again new territories: they attract, they invoke, they call forth. The same happens with thoughts: you are enchanted with one sort of thinking, but by the time you become acquainted with it the honeymoon is over, the love is over. Now you would like to be interested in something else, something new that again gives you a thrill, a kick. This way one goes from one woman to another, from one man to another. This sort of searching will never allow you enough time to create trust.

The Playboy

> Is this a blessing? After being alone for a long time, I fell in love with three women at the same time, which was easy in the beginning. But as soon as I started to get into a deeper relationship with one, either I ran to the next one or the first one wanted to be with someone else. Of course the same happened again as soon as I got in tune with one of the other women. So joy and suffering are pretty close together, but I wonder – am I avoiding something?

Don't you think three are more than enough? Do you think you are avoiding the fourth? One woman is enough to create hell, and you are asking me, "Is this a blessing?" It must be a curse in disguise.

"What has happened to Jack? I have not seen him for ages."
"Oh, he married the girl he rescued from drowning."
"And is he happy?"
"You bet! But he hates water now."

You must be a great soul – either so unconscious that even three women cannot create any trouble for you, or so enlightened that "who cares?"

While riding home from work one evening, three commuters became friendly in the lounge car and, after the third round, they began to brag about the relative merits of their respective marital relationships.

The first proudly proclaimed, “My wife meets my train every evening and we've been married for ten years.”

“That's nothing,” scoffed the second. “My wife meets me every evening, too, and we've been married for seventeen years.”

“Well, I have got you both beat, fellows,” said the third commuter, who was obviously the youngest in the group.

“How do you figure that?” the first fellow wanted to know.

“I suppose you have a wife who meets you every evening, too!” sneered the second.

“That's right,” said the third commuter, “and I'm not even married.”

Three women, and you are not even married! They will make a football of you. And you are asking, “Is this a blessing?” – with a question mark of course. Be a little more careful: this is a dangerous place for people like you. There are so many women here, and if you go on like this soon nothing will be left of you, and I will unnecessarily lose a disciple. Think of me too!

Weinstein, a very wealthy businessman, had an unattractive daughter. He found a young man to marry her and after ten years they had two children.

Weinstein called his son-in-law into the office one day. “Listen,” he said, “you have given me two beautiful grandchildren, you have made me very happy. I am gonna give you forty-nine percent of the business.”

“Thank you, Pop!”

“Is there anything else I could do for you?”

“Yeah, buy me out!”

I am ready to buy you out whatever the price. Just inquire of the three women!

Love is significant, a good learning situation, but only a learning situation. One school is enough, three schools are too many. And with three women you will not be able to learn much, you will be in such turmoil. It is better to be with one so that you can be more totally one with her, so that you can understand her and your own longings more clearly, so you are less clouded, less in anguish – because love in the beginning is only an unconscious phenomenon. It is biological, it is nothing very precious. Only when you bring your awareness to it, when you become more and more meditative about it, does it start becoming precious, it starts soaring high.

Intimacy with one woman or one man is better than having many superficial relationships. Love is not a seasonal flower, it takes years to grow. And only when it grows does it go beyond biology and start having something of the spiritual in it. Just being with many women or many men will keep you superficial – entertained maybe, but superficial; occupied certainly, but that occupation is not going to help in inward growth.

But a one-to-one relationship, a sustained relationship so that you can understand each other more closely, is tremendously beneficial. Why is it so? And what is the need to understand the woman or the man? The need is because every man has a feminine part in his being, and every woman has a masculine part in her being. The only way to understand it, the easiest way to understand it, the most natural way to understand it, is to be in deep, intimate relationship with someone. If you are a man be in a deep, intimate relationship with a woman. Let trust grow so all barriers dissolve. Come so close to each other that you can look deep into the woman and the woman can look deep into you. Don't be dishonest with each other.

And if you are having so many relationships you will be dishonest, you will be lying continually. You will have to lie, you will have to be insincere, you will have to say things which you don't mean – and they will all suspect. It is very difficult to create trust with a woman if you are having some other relationship. It is easy to deceive a man because he lives through the intellect; it is very difficult, almost impossible to deceive a woman because she lives intuitively. You will not be able to look directly into her eyes; you will be afraid that she may start reading your soul, and you are hiding so many deceptive things, so many dishonesties.

So if you are having many relationships, you will not be able to dive deep into the psyche of the woman. And that is the only thing that is needed: to know your own inner feminine part. A relationship becomes a mirror. The woman starts looking into you and starts finding her own masculine part; the man looks into the woman and starts discovering his own femininity. And the more you become aware of your feminine, the other pole, the more whole you can be, the more integrated you can be. When your inner man and your inner woman have disappeared into each other, have become dissolved into each other, when they are no longer separate, when they have become one integrated whole, you have become an individual. Carl Gustav Jung calls it the process of individuation. He is right, he has chosen the right word for it. And the same happens to a woman.

But playing with many people will keep you superficial – entertained, occupied, but not growing; and the only thing that matters ultimately is growth, the growth of integration, individuality, the growth of a center in you. That growth needs you to know your other part. The easiest approach is to know the woman on the outside first, so that you can know the woman inside.

Just like a mirror – the mirror reflects your face, it shows you your face – the woman becomes your mirror, the man becomes your mirror. The other reflects your face, but if you have so many mirrors around you, running from one mirror to another and deceiving each mirror about the other, you will be in a chaos, you will go nuts.

At the lowest, love is a kind of politics, power politics. Wherever love is contaminated by the idea of domination, it is politics. Whether you call it politics or not is not the question, it is political. And millions of people never know anything about love except this politics – the politics that exists between husbands and wives, boyfriends and girlfriends. It is politics, the whole thing is political: you want to dominate the other, you enjoy domination. And love is nothing but politics sugar-coated, a bitter pill sugar-coated. You talk about love, but the deep desire is to exploit the other. And I am not saying that you are doing it deliberately or consciously – you are not that conscious yet. You cannot do it deliberately; it is an unconscious mechanism.

The Boyfriend

> My girlfriend told me I am a little boring, not very juicy, very dependent and a victim. I observed in me this destructive energy and I felt that I somehow enjoyed it! Is it possible to use this energy in some creative way?

Your girlfriend is very compassionate, because each man finally becomes *very* boring, not a little boring. Do you realize the fact that what you call love is a repetition, the same stupid gymnastics again and again? And in this whole stupid game the man is the loser. He is dissipating his energy, perspiring, huffing, puffing, and the girl keeps her eyes closed, thinking, "It is a question only of two or three minutes and this nightmare will be finished."

People are so non-inventive that they take it for granted that going through the same actions is making them more interesting. That's why I say your girlfriend is very compassionate – she only told you that you are a little boring. I say to you, you are *utterly* boring.

When the Christian missionaries came to India, people discovered that they knew only one posture of making love – the woman underneath and those ugly beasts on top of the delicate woman. In India that posture is called the "missionary posture." India is an ancient land and the birth place of many sciences, particularly sexology. A book of tremendous importance, by Vatsyayana, has been in existence for five thousand years. The name of the book is *Kamasutra*, hints for making love. And it comes from a man of deep meditation – he has created eighty-four postures for love-making. Naturally the love posture should change; otherwise you are bound to be boring.

Vatsyayana recognizes the fact that the same love posture creates boredom, a feeling of utter stupidity, because you are always doing the same thing. He invented eighty-four postures to make the love life of couples a little interesting. Nobody in the whole world has written a book of the caliber of *Kamasutra*. But it could only have come from a man of immense clarity, of deep meditativeness.

What is your lovemaking? If you look at your lovemaking, you yourself will feel that it is all boring. And particularly for the woman it is more boring, because the man is finished in two or three minutes and the woman has not even started. And all around the world, cultures have enforced in the minds of women that they are not supposed even to enjoy or move or be playful – that is called "dirty"; prostitutes do it, not ladies. Ladies have to lie down almost dead and let that old guy do whatever he wants to do; it is nothing new, there is nothing new even to see.

You should not take it as a personal disrespect. Your girlfriend is telling you something really sincere and honest. Have you given her orgasmic joy, or have you only used her to throw out your sexual energy? Have you reduced her to a commodity? She has been conditioned to accept it, but even this accepting cannot be joyful.

You make love on the same bed where you fight every day. In fact fighting is the preface: throwing pillows, shouting at each other, arguing about everything and then, feeling tired, some negotiation is needed. Your love is only a negotiation. If you are a man of aesthetic sensibility your love chamber should be a sacred place, because it is in that love chamber that life is born. It should have beautiful flowers, incense, fragrance; you should enter it with deep respect.

And love should not be just an abrupt thing – grab the woman. This hit-and-run affair is not love. Love should have a preface of beautiful music, of dancing together, of meditating together. And love should not be a mind thing – that you are continuously thinking of how to make love and then go to sleep. Love should be a deeper involvement of your whole being and it should not be projected by the mind, but should come out spontaneously. Beautiful music, fragrance, you are dancing hand in hand, you have again become small children playing with flowers. If love happens spontaneously in this sacred atmosphere it will have a different quality.

You should understand that the woman is capable of multiple orgasms because she does not lose any energy. Man is capable of only one orgasm and he loses energy, looks depressed. Even the next morning you can see his hangover, and as he goes on growing older it becomes more and more difficult. This difference has to be understood. The woman is on the receptive end – she has to be because she has to become a mother, she needs more energy. But her orgasm has a totally different way of happening. Man's sexuality is local, like local anesthesia. A woman's body is sexual all over, and unless her whole body starts trembling with joy, each cell of her body starts becoming involved, she cannot have an orgasmic explosion.

So it is not only in your case, it is the case for almost ninety-nine percent of women around the world. The whole situation has to be changed. The woman should not be under the man. In the first place it is ugly – man has a stronger body, the woman is more fragile. She should be on top of the man, not the man on top of the woman.

Secondly, man should remain silent, inactive, so that his orgasm is not finished within two minutes. If you are silent and let the woman go crazy on top of your chest, it will give her good exercise and it will bring her to an explosion of orgasmic energy. It takes time for her whole body to warm up, and if you are not inactive there is no time. So you meet, but the meeting is not of beauty, of love, but just utilitarian.

Try what I am saying with your girlfriend. Be the inactive partner and let her be the active partner. Allow her to be uninhibited. She has not to behave like a lady, she has to behave like an authentic woman. The lady is just created by man; woman is created by existence. You have to fill the gap between her orgasms. The gap can be filled in only one way, that you remain very inactive, silent, and enjoy her going crazy. And she will have multiple orgasms. You should end the game with your orgasm, but you should not begin with it.

And your woman will not call you a little boring. You will be a really interesting, real wonderful guy who is behaving like a lady! Keep your eyes closed so that she is not inhibited by your eyes. So she can do anything – movement of the hands, movement of the body, moaning, groaning, shouting. Until she says, "*Hari om tat sat!*" you are not allowed to be alive, you simply remain silent. This should be the indication. "*Hari om tat sat*" simply means: this orgasmic explosion, this is the truth. Then she will be mad after you. Right now you must be behaving stupidly, as most of the men in the world do.

The second thing you say: "My girlfriend is saying that I am not very juicy." So become a little more juicy! To become juicy is not very difficult. The juice of all kinds of fruits is available everywhere. Drink more juice, less solid food. She is giving you good advice and you in your stupidity are thinking that she is condemning you.

When she says, "You are very dependent and a victim," I can see even through your question that she is right. You are victim, just as every human being is a victim – a victim of stupid ideologies which have created strange guilt feelings and do not allow you to be playful. Although you may be making love, you know you are committing a sin and that hell is not far off.

Becky Goldberg was telling her husband Hymie, "You are a great lover!"

Goldberg said, "But you never told me this before. I was waiting for somebody to say that I am a great lover, but I dropped the idea because it seems I am not."

Becky Goldberg said to him, "No, you are a great lover, and I wanted to say it to you many times, but you were not there!"

Making love to Becky...and Goldberg is not there. He is counting his money, doing his accounts, and his mind is doing thousands of things. In every bed where there are two lovers, there are at least – I mean minimum – four people. There are more inventive people, they may have a whole crowd in the bed. The woman is making love to Goldberg and thinking of Muhammad Ali. Goldberg is making love as a duty and is thinking of so many beautiful actresses; but his mind is not there, and neither is his wife's mind there. Their minds are in their dreams.

A man told his friend, "Last night I had a tremendous dream. I have to tell you. I have been waiting for the morning to tell you the dream."

The man said, "What kind of dream?"

He said, "I went fishing in my dream and I caught such big fish that even to draw in one big fish was a strenuous job for me. And I caught so many fish! I don't know where these fish disappear to in the day."

The other man said, "Stop all this nonsense, you don't know what I have dreamed. I found in my dream, on one side of me,

Sophia Loren, absolutely nude. And I said, 'My God, have I reached heaven?' And on the other side was another beautiful woman. It was impossible to judge who was more beautiful."

The other friend became very angry and he said, "You idiot! You pretend to be my best friend. Why didn't you call me?"

He said, "I did call, but your wife said you had gone fishing."

Nobody is where you think he is. Nobody is at home.

While making love, make it a meditative process. Your whole presence has to be there, showering on the woman you love. The woman has to be there, showering all her beauty and grace on her lover. Then you will not be a victim, otherwise you are a victim.

Love is not accepted by your so-called, utterly idiotic, religions to be a natural and playful experience. They condemn it. They have made it a condition: unless you leave your woman you will never attain truth. And the conditioning has been going on for so long that it has almost become a truth, although it is an absolute lie. You are a victim of traditions and you are certainly dependent.

You are saying, "I observed in me this destructive energy and I felt that I somehow enjoyed it." Everybody has destructive energy because energy is bound to be destructive, if left to itself – unless it is used with awareness and becomes creative.

But the most important thing that you are saying is that, "Somehow I enjoyed it." Then how are you going to change it? With anything that you enjoy you are bound to remain on the same level; you cannot change it because you may not enjoy the change. You have energy. To enjoy destructive energy is suicidal, to enjoy destructive energy as destructive is in the service of death. If you are aware of it you have to go through a transformation. Use your energy creatively. Perhaps that will make you less boring, more juicy, less dependent, less of a victim.

And the most important part will be that you will not feel guilty and depressed. No creative person feels depressed and guilty. His participation in the universe by his creative actions makes him tremendously fulfilled and gives him dignity. That is the very birthright of every man, but very few people claim it.

And there is no difficulty, it is so easy to use energy in creative fields. Paint, do gardening, grow flowers, write poetry, learn music, dance. Learn anything that changes your destructive energy into creative energy. Then you will not be angry at existence, you will be grateful. You will not be against life. How can a creative person be against life, love? It is impossible, it has never happened. It is only the uncreative people who are against everything.

Your girl has raised very important questions for your life. The easiest way would be to change the girlfriend, but I suggest that your girlfriend is certainly a friend to you and that whatever she has said is absolutely sincere, authentic. Be grateful to her and start changing things. The day your girlfriend accepts you as juicy, as interesting, will be a great day in your life. So don't be a coward and change girlfriends just because this girlfriend creates trouble in your mind, and you want to find some other girlfriend.

You are fortunate to find a very compassionate girl. Your next choice will be very difficult; she will make you feel absolutely guilty and unworthy. Because what have you done to be worthy? What have you done not to be boring? What have you done to declare your independence? What have you done not to be a victim? It is time you should do it. You will remain always grateful to your girlfriend.

I would like to tell your girlfriend, "Go on hitting this fellow until you are satisfied that he is not boring, but full of juice, utterly interesting, playful, celebrating. You may lose him somewhere on the path of life, but you will have prepared him for some other woman; otherwise the way he is now, he is going to torture many women and torture himself."

A woman is a mystery, so is a man. Don't call her your wife; she is not yours. And she is not a wife. A wife is a function! That is not her totality; she is many more things. She is not finished by being a wife. She may be a painter, she may be a singer, she may be a dancer. She may be a thousand and one things! Why call her just a wife? "Wife" is just a function.

The Husband

> I am a married man with three children and with all the problems of a married man's life. My wife is constantly at my throat. We are together only for the sake of the children; otherwise, each moment is a nightmare. Is there any chance of my escaping hellfire?

I will tell you a story:

A man was arraigned before an Arkansas justice on a charge of obtaining money under false pretenses. The judge looked at him thoughtfully. "Your name is Jim Moore?"

"Yes, sir."

"You are charged with a crime that merits a long term in the penitentiary?"

"Yes, sir."

"You are guilty of that crime?"

The man squared his shoulders doggedly: "I am."

"You ask me for mercy?"

"No, sir."

The judge smiled grimly. "You have had a great deal of trouble within the last two years?"

"I have."

"You have often wished you were dead?"

"I have...please, Your Honor."

"You wanted to steal enough money to take you far away from Arkansas?"

"You are right, Judge."

"If a man had stepped up and shot you as you entered the

store, you would have said, 'Thank you, sir'?"

"Why, yes, I would. But, Judge, how in the world did you find out so much about me?"

"Some time ago," said the Judge, with a solemn air, "I divorced my wife. Shortly afterward you married her. The result is conclusive. I discharge you. Here, take this fifty-dollar bill. You have suffered enough."

You need not be worried about hell: you have suffered enough, you are already in it! You can only go to heaven because nothing else is left. Celibates may go to hell, but you cannot. You have suffered enough. Celibates may need a little taste of suffering, but not you.

In fact, there is no hell somewhere else and no heaven either. Hell is here, heaven is here. Hell and heaven are your ways of being. They are your ways of living. You can live in such a way that the whole of life is a benediction. But don't go on throwing the responsibility only on your wife. In the first place it is you who have chosen her. Why have you chosen such a wife who is constantly at your neck?

And do you think, if you are divorced, you will not again choose another woman of the same type? If you ask psychologists they will say you will again choose the same type of woman. You needed it; it is your own choice. You cannot live without misery. You think your wife is creating the misery? It is because you wanted to live in misery; that's why you have chosen this woman. You will again choose the same type of woman. You will only become attracted to the same type of woman unless you drop your old mind completely.

Except our own minds, there is no other way to change or transform. You must be thinking that if you divorce this woman things will be good. You are wrong, you are utterly wrong. You don't know a thing about human psychology. You will get trapped again. You will search for a woman again; you will miss this woman very much. She will miss you, you will miss her. You will again find the same type of person; you will be attracted only to that kind of person.

Watch your mind. And then, only she cannot be at fault; you must be doing something to her too. The question is your statement; I don't know her statement. It will be unfair to the poor woman if I accept your statement about her totally. You may be fifty percent right, but what about the other fifty percent? You must be supplying fuel to the fire. And if life was so ugly, why have you given birth to three children? Who is responsible for that? Why have you brought three souls into the ugly world of your family, into the nightmare that you are living? Why? Can't you have any love for your children?

People go on reproducing without thinking at all of what they are doing. If your life is such a hell, at least you could have prevented your children from falling into the trap of your misery. You would have saved them! Now those three children are being brought up by two persons like you and your wife. They will learn ways and means from you, and they will perpetuate you in the world. When you are gone, you will still be here in the world creating hell. Those children will perpetuate, they will keep the continuity of your stupid ways of living, miserable ways of living.

Now your boy will find a woman just like your wife – who else? – because he will know only this woman. He will love his mother, and whenever he falls in love with a woman it simply means that woman reminds him of his mother. Now again the same game will be played. Maybe you have chosen your wife according to your mother; your father and your mother were playing the same game that you are playing, and your children will perpetuate the same structure and the same gestalt. That's how miseries persist.

At least you could have saved these three children's lives, and you could have saved the future of humanity, because the ripple that you have created will go on and on. Even when you are gone it will be there. Whatever you do abides. Whatever ripples you create in the ocean of life remain. You disappear – it is like throwing a stone into a silent lake. The stone falls deep into the lake, disappears, goes to the bottom and rests there, but the ripples that have been created; they go on spreading toward the shores. And the ocean of life knows no shores, so those waves go on and on, forever and forever. At least you could have been a little more alert not to produce children.

But it is never too late. Still, life can be changed – but don' t hope that your wife should change. That is the wrong approach. *You* change. Change radically. Stop doing things that you have always been doing. Start doing things that you have never done. Change radically, become a new person, and you will be surprised: when you become a new person, your wife becomes a new person. She will have to, to respond to you. In the beginning she will find it hard because it will be almost like living with another husband. But slowly, slowly she will see that if you can change, why can't she?

Never hope that the other should change. In every relationship, start the change from your side. Life can still become a paradise; it is never too late. But great courage is needed to change.

All that is really needed is a little more awareness.

De-automatize your behavior; just watch what you have been doing up to now. You do the same thing, and the wife reacts in the same way. It has become a settled pattern. Watch any husband and wife – they are almost predictable. In the morning the husband will spread his newspaper and start reading, and the wife will say the same thing that she has been saying for years, and the husband will react in the same way. It has become almost structured, programmed.

Just small changes, and you will be surprised. Tomorrow, don't sit in your chair early in the morning and start reading your paper. Just start cleaning the house, and see what happens. Your wife will be wide-eyed, and she will not be able to believe what has happened to you. Smile when you see your wife, hug her, and see how she is taken aback. You have never hugged her. Years have passed, and you have never looked into the poor woman's eyes.

Tonight, just sit in front of her, look into her eyes. She will think in the beginning that you have gone crazy, you have become an Osho freak or something, but don't be worried. Just hold her hand and be ecstatic. If you cannot be, at least pretend. Be ecstatic. Sometimes it happens that if you start pretending, it starts happening! Just start smiling, for no reason at all, and watch. Your poor woman may have a heart attack!

You have not been holding her hand – do you remember since how long? Have you ever taken her for a morning walk? Or when the moon is full, have you taken her for a walk in the night under the stars? She is also human, she also needs love. But, and in India particularly, people go on using women as if they are just servants. Their whole work consists of taking care of the children and the kitchen and the house, as if that's their whole life. Have you respected your wife as a human being? Then, if anger arises, it is natural. If she feels frustrated it is because her life is running out and she has not known any joy, she has not known any bliss, she has not known anything that can give meaning and significance to her life.

Have you just sat by her side sometimes, silently, just holding her hand, not saying a word, just feeling her and letting her feel you? Wives and husbands have only one kind of communication: quarreling. Don't think that only your wife is responsible. She may be, but that is not the point because she has not asked the question. You have asked the question. Start changing your life. Give the poor woman a little feeling of significance. Give the little woman a little feeling that she is needed. Do you know the greatest need in life is to be needed? And unless a person feels that he or she is needed, his or her life remains meaningless, desertlike.

Laugh with her, listen to music together, go for a holiday. Caress her body, because bodies start shrinking when nobody caresses them. Bodies start becoming ugly when nobody looks with appreciation. And then you think, "Why is my wife not beautiful?" You are not creating the climate in which beauty flowers, blooms. If you love a person, the person immediately becomes beautiful! Love is such an alchemical process. Look at a person with loving eyes and suddenly you will see his or her aura changing, the face becoming radiant, more blood coming to the face, eyes becoming more shiny, radiance, intelligence – and like a miracle!

Love is a miracle, love is magical. It is not yet too late.

You may be surprised to know that the word uncle *is older than the word* father, *because matriarchy preceded patriarchy. The mother was there and the father was not known because the mother was meeting, merging, melting with many people. Somebody had to be the father, but there was no way to find out. So all were uncles – all potential fathers were uncles. The institution of fatherhood came into existence with the invention of private property; they are joined together. The father represents private property, because when private property came into existence everybody wanted his own child to inherit it. "I will not be here, but a part of me should inherit my property."*
Private property came first, then came the father.

The Father

Christianity, I have been told by Christian friends, is based on the family: the family is its foundation stone. But the family is also the foundation stone of all neurosis, of all psychosis, of all kinds of mental sicknesses, of all kinds of social problems. It is also the base of races, of nations, of wars.

The family has to be understood. It has no future; it has already outlived its usefulness, its necessity. But we have been conditioned – not only Christians, but everybody – that the family is a great contribution to the world. The reality is totally different. I have to go point by point, in detail, because the problem of family is one of the most serious problems.

The first thing.... The family is a prison; it wants to keep control of the children, of the wife. It is a very tight group of people, and they have made this prison sacred. But the results are very ugly. Every kind of imprisonment prevents spiritual growth. What do you think: why did Buddha renounce the world? Why did Mahavira renounce the world? In fact they were not renouncing the world, they were simply renouncing the family – nobody has said this before – because how can you renounce the world? Wherever you are, the world is. You can only renounce the family. But all religious scriptures, including Christian scriptures, are continuously lying to people: they talk of renouncing the world. It distracts you completely from the fact that all these people were renouncing the *family*, because the family was such that they could not grow within it.

The family is programming every child according to its prejudices. If you are born into a Christian family you will be continuously programmed for Christianity, and you will not ever suspect that your conditioning may be wrong, your conditioning may be preventing you from going beyond.

Christianity and all other religions go on confusing people's minds. They never make the distinction between believing and knowing. A blind man can believe in light, but that is not going to help. One needs eyes to see the light, and then there is no need to believe. When you *know* something, is there any need to believe in it?

Do you "believe" in light? Do you believe in the moon? Do you believe in the stars? You simply know, there is no question of belief. Belief arises only for fictions, for lies, not for truth. Every belief system is a hindrance for spirituality.

Death, according to Christianity, is a taboo: you should not talk about it. Death is taboo and life is also taboo: you should not live it! Death you should not talk about, and life you should not live! They don't leave you any alternative – you can neither live, nor can you die. They keep you hanging in the middle, half-dead, half-alive.

This creates schizophrenia. You are not allowed to be total in anything: in life, in death, in love, you are only partially involved. A man who is partially involved is only partially alive. The deeper your involvement in existence, the deeper your life. When you are involved totally in life, in death, in love, in meditation, in any kind of thing that you want to do, painting, music, poetry, dance... Unless you are totally involved in it you will never know the maximum, the optimum pleasure, the optimum blissfulness.

People are living only at the minimum, just surviving – or, to be absolutely truthful, just vegetating, just waiting and waiting, and nothing happens in their life. No flowers blossom in their life, no festivals happen in their life. And their death is as ugly as their life was, because death is the ultimate culmination of your life.

If you have lived totally, death is not the end. Death is only an episode, a small episode in an eternal life. You have died many times, but because you have never lived totally you became unconscious at the moment of death; the fear brought you into a coma. That's why you don't remember your past lives – because the coma stands as a barrier for the past lives and their remembrance. And because you don't know your past lives you cannot understand that there is going to be life after death, that life is eternal. Birth and death are mere episodes; thousands of times you have been into birth, into death. But when you are not allowed to live totally, when everywhere there is interference from religion...

On his first day at school a small boy – of course a Christian boy – was asked by the teacher, "What is your name?"

He said, "Don't."

The teacher said, "Strange, I have never heard such a name."

He said, "Everything, whatever I do, I only hear this: 'Don't' – so I think it is my name."

But the whole of Christianity is doing that to everybody. It is a life-negative religion, it does not allow you to live joyously. And the family is the root because obviously the programming starts from the family. Christianity says that it is founded on the family. And I know perfectly well that unless the family disappears from the world these religions, these nations, these wars will not disappear because they are all based on the family.

The family teaches you that you are a Hindu, and the Hindu religion is the best religion of all; other religions are so-so. Christianity continues the programming of children: "You can be saved only through Jesus Christ. Nobody else can save you. All other religions are just moralities, very superficial, they are not going to help you." And when a child, alongside his breast feeding, is continuously fed with all kinds of superstitions – God, and the Holy Ghost and the only begotten son of God, Jesus, heaven and hell... Children are very vulnerable because they are born as a tabula rasa – nothing is written on them, their minds are pure. You can write anything you want on the child. And every family commits the crime: they destroy the individual and create a slave. Obedience is virtue, disobedience is the original sin.

When a child starts being programmed from his very birth, when he is very vulnerable and very soft, you can write anything. It will go on in his unconscious. You can tell him that "Our nation is the greatest nation in the world"; every nation is saying that. "Our religion is the greatest religion, our scripture is written by God himself" – the Hindus are saying that, the Christians are saying that, the Jews are saying that. Everybody is committing the same crime.

Christianity, of course, is doing it more efficiently, more cunningly, because it is the biggest religion in the world. It uses ultramodern techniques of programming. It sends its missionaries to learn psychoanalysis, to learn how to program people, how to deprogram people. If a Hindu has to be converted to Christianity, first he has to be deprogrammed of Hinduism. Again the tabula rasa appears; what was written is erased. Now you can write, "Christianity is the highest religion in the world, and there has been no man like Jesus Christ, and will never be again, because he is the only begotten son of God."

All wars depend on the family. It has been a tradition in many nations in the past that you contribute at least one son to the army to protect the nation, to protect the dignity and the pride of the nation. In Tibet, every family has to contribute the eldest son to the monasteries. This has been done for thousands of years. As if the children are just commodities you can contribute, as if the children are money you can give to charity!

This divided the world into different camps because of religion, because of politics, because of nationalities, because of race. They all depend on the family. The family is the root cause of mankind's thousands of wounds.

The family gives you ambition, it gives you desires, it gives you a longing to be successful, and all these things create your tensions, your anxieties: how to be a celebrity? The family wants you to be a celebrity. The family wants you to be known all over the world. The family wants you to be the richest person. The family wants you to be the president of the country. All these ambitions the family creates, without knowing that all these ambitions are creating a mind which will remain continuously in anguish, suffering. Only one man can become the president of the country – what about the other hundreds of million people in the country? They are all failures? This is an ugly situation, to keep people feeling they are failures, unsuccessful, inferior to others.

The family is the base for all pathology.

I would love a world where the family is replaced by the commune. Psychologically it is more healthy to have a commune, where children are not possessed by the parents; they belong to the commune. Where children are not given the imprint of only the mother and father – they have many uncles in the commune, many aunts in the commune. Sometimes they sleep with this family, sometimes with that family. I want the family to be replaced by the commune.

It is one of the strangest phenomena that for thousands of years, men and women have been living together, yet they are strangers. They go on giving birth to children, but still they remain strangers. The feminine approach and the masculine approach are so opposed to each other that unless a conscious effort is made, unless it becomes your meditation, there is no hope of having a peaceful life.

It is one of my deep concerns: how to make love and meditation so involved in each other that each love affair automatically becomes a partnership in meditation – and each meditation makes you so conscious that you need not fall in love, you can rise in love. You can find a friend consciously, deliberately.

The Friend

> My love-life drama now reflects an old saying of Humphrey Bogart's: "Women – they're hell to live with, and hell to live without." What to do?

One has to pass through this hell. One has to experience both the hell of living with a woman and the hell of living without a woman. And it is not only true about women, it is absolutely true about men too. So don't be a male chauvinist pig! It is applicable both ways, it is a double-edged sword. Women are also tired of living with men, and they are also frustrated when they have to live alone. It is one of the most fundamental of human dilemmas; it has to be understood. You cannot live without a woman because you don't know how to live with yourself. You are not meditative enough.

Meditation is the art of living with yourself. It is nothing else than that, simply that: the art of being joyously alone. A meditator can sit joyously alone for months, for years. He does not hanker for the other because his own inner ecstasy is so much, is so overpowering, who bothers about the other? If the other comes into his life it is not a need, it is a luxury. And I am all for luxury because luxury means you can enjoy it if it is there, and you can enjoy it when it is not there. A need is a difficult phenomenon. For example, bread and butter are needs, but the flowers in the garden are a luxury. You can live without the flowers, you will not die, but you cannot live without bread and butter.

For the man who cannot live with himself, the other is a need, an absolute need, because whenever he is alone he is bored with himself – so bored that he wants some occupation with somebody else.

Because it is a need, it becomes a dependence; you have to depend on the other. And because it becomes a dependence, you hate, you rebel, you resist because it is a slavery. Dependence is a kind of slavery and nobody wants to be a slave.

You meet a woman – you are not able to live alone, the woman is also not able to live alone. That's why she is meeting you; otherwise there is no need. Both are bored with themselves, and both are thinking that the other will help to get rid of the boredom. Yes, in the beginning it looks like that – but only in the beginning. As they settle together, soon they see that the boredom is not destroyed – it is not only doubled but multiplied! First they were bored with themselves, now they are bored with the other, too – because the closer you come to the other, the more you know the other, the more the other becomes almost a part of you. That's why if you see a bored couple walking by, you can be certain they are married. If they are not bored, you can be certain they are not married. The man must be walking with somebody else's wife, that's why there is so much joy.

When you are in love – when you have not yet persuaded the woman, and the woman has not yet persuaded you to be together forever – you both pretend great joy. And something of it is true, too, because of the hope, "Who knows, I may come out of my boredom, my anguish, my anxiety, my aloneness. This woman may help me." And the woman is also hoping. But once you are together, the hopes soon disappear. Despair sets in again. Now you are bored and the problem has multiplied. Now how to get rid of this woman?

Because you are not meditative you need others to keep you occupied. And because you are not meditative you are not able to love, either, because love is an overflowing joy. You are bored with yourself; what have you got to share with the other? Hence, being with the other also becomes hell.

In that sense Jean-Paul Sartre is right that "The other is hell." The other is not hell, really; it only appears so. The hell exists in you, in your non-meditativeness, in your incapacity to be alone and ecstatic. And both are unable to be alone and ecstatic; now both are at each other's throats, continuously trying to snatch some happiness from each other. Both are doing that and both are beggars.

I have heard...

One psychoanalyst met another psychoanalyst on the street.

The first said to the other, "You look fine. How am I?"

Nobody knows about himself, nobody is acquainted with himself. We only see others' faces. A woman looks beautiful, a man looks beautiful, smiling, all smiles. We don't know his anguish. Maybe all those smiles are just a facade to deceive others and to deceive himself. Maybe behind those smiles there are great tears. Maybe he is afraid if he does not smile he may start weeping and crying. When you see the other you simply see the surface; you fall in love with the surface. But when you come closer you soon know that the inner depths of the other person are as dark as your own. He is a beggar just as you are. Now two beggars begging from each other. Then it becomes hell.

Yes, you are right: "Women – they're hell to live with, and hell to live without." It is not a question of women at all, nor a question of men; it is a question of meditation and love. Meditation is the source from which joy wells up within you and starts overflowing. If you have joy enough to share, only then will your love be a contentment. If you don't have joy enough to share, your love is going to be tiring, exhausting, boring. So whenever you are with a woman you are bored and you want to get rid of her, and whenever you are alone you are bored with yourself and you want to get rid of your loneliness, and you seek and search for a woman. This is a vicious circle! You can go on moving like a pendulum from one extreme to the other your whole life.

See the real problem. The real problem has nothing to do with man and woman. The real problem has something to do with meditation and the flowering of meditation in love, in joy, in blissfulness.

First meditate, be blissful, then much love will happen of its own accord. Then being with others is beautiful, and being alone is also beautiful. Then it is simple, too. You don't depend on others and you don't make others dependent on you. Then it is always a friendship, a friendliness. It never becomes a relationship, it is always a relatedness. You relate, but you don't create a marriage. Marriage is out of fear, relatedness is out of love.

You relate; as long as things are moving beautifully, you share. And if you see that the moment has come to depart because your paths separate at this crossroad, you say good-bye with great gratitude for all that the other has been to you, for all the joys and all the pleasures and all the beautiful moments that you have shared with the other. With no misery, with no pain, you simply separate.

Nobody can guarantee that two persons will be happy together always because people change. When you meet a woman she is one person, you are one person. After ten years you will be another person, she will be another person. It is like a river: the water is continuously flowing. The people who had fallen in love are no longer there, both are no longer there. Now you can go on clinging to a certain promise given by somebody else, but *you* had not given it.

A real man of understanding never promises for tomorrow. He can only say "for the moment." A really sincere man cannot promise at all. How can he promise? Who knows about tomorrow? Tomorrow may come, may not come. Tomorrow may come: "I will not be the same, you will not be the same." Tomorrow may come: "You may find somebody with whom you fit more deeply, I may find somebody whom I go with more harmoniously." The world is vast. Why exhaust it today? Keep the doors open, keep alternatives open.

I am against marriage. It is marriage that creates problems. It is marriage that has become very ugly. Marriage is the most ugly institution in the world because it forces people to be phony: they have changed, but they go on pretending that they are the same.

One old man, eighty years old, was celebrating his fiftieth wedding anniversary with his wife who was seventy-five. They went to the same hotel, to the same resort where they had gone on their honeymoon. The nostalgia! Now he is eighty, she is seventy-five. They booked into the same hotel and took the same room as last time. They were trying to live those beautiful days of fifty years ago again.

When they were going to sleep, the woman said, "Have you forgotten? Aren't you going to kiss me the way you kissed me on our honeymoon night?"

The old man said, "Okay," and got up.

The woman asked, "Where are you going?"

He said, "I am going to get my teeth from the bathroom."

Everything has changed. Now this kiss, without teeth or with false teeth, is not going to be the same kiss. But the man says, "Okay." The journey must have been tiring, and for an eighty-year-old... But people go on behaving as if they were the same.

Very few people really grow up; even if they become aged they don't grow up. Growing old is not growing up. Real maturity comes through meditation.

Learn to be silent, peaceful, still. Learn to be a no-mind. That has to be the beginning. Nothing can be done before that, and everything becomes easier after that. When you find yourself utterly happy and blissful, then even if the third world war happens and the whole world disappears leaving you alone, it won't affect you. You will be still sitting under your tree and meditating.

The day that moment comes in your life, you can share your joy – now you are able to give love. Before that it is going to be misery, hopes and frustrations, desires and failures, dreams...and then dust in your hand and in your mouth. Beware, don't waste time. The earlier you become attuned to no-mind, the better it is. Then many things can flower in you: love, creativity, spontaneity, joy, prayer, gratitude, godliness.

Part 3

ADAM IN THE WORLD

In the day be active, in the night, sleep. Action and meditation should be together. That is why I never suggest to anybody to move to the Himalayas and renounce the world, because then you will be simply lazy and sleeping: again imbalance. Be in the world but when you come to your home, really come to your home; leave the office, leave it behind. Don't carry the files in your head. When you are inactive, enjoy inactivity, and when you are active, enjoy activity, and let the body feel and move according to Tao, not according to your mind.

All ambition arises out of an inferiority complex. It is very rare to come across a politician who is intelligent. It is very rare to come across a rich person who is intelligent, very, very difficult – because an intelligent person, by his very intelligence, becomes noncompetitive. Intelligence is noncompetitive, intelligence can see the whole absurdity of it. Intelligence can see "I am myself and there is no need to compare myself with anybody else. I am neither higher nor lower. Not that I am just like the others. I am different, but there is no higher and lower." We are all different and unique human beings, but nobody is lower and nobody is higher – and the whole effort to become higher is stupid.

The Politician

I am a radical revolutionary politician. Have you something to say to me?

You have already gone too far – you will not listen. Just to be a politician is enough, but you are a revolutionary radical politician – cancer doubled, trebled! Is not politics enough? Have you to be radical, revolutionary? But we always find beautiful words to hide ugly realities.

No politician can be revolutionary because the only revolution is spiritual. No politician can be radical either; the very word *radical* means concerning the roots. The politician only prunes the leaves, he has nothing to do with the roots. Only enlightenment takes you to the roots, only meditation takes you to the roots of the problems.

Politics has existed always, politicians have existed always, but what has happened? The world remains the same sorry-go-round! In fact, misery goes on becoming multiplied every day. All these revolutionaries and radical politicians have only proved to be mischievous – with good intentions, of course, but intentions don't count at all. What counts is consciousness.

The politician has no consciousness; in fact, he is trying to avoid his own inner problems, he is trying to escape from his own problems. And the easiest way to escape from oneself is to become concerned about world problems, economics, politics, history, service to the poor, transformation of the conditions of the society, reformation. All these are strategies for escaping from one's own problems – subtle strategies, dangerous, because one feels that one is doing something great, while one is simply being a coward.

First face your own problems, encounter them. First try to transform *your* being. Only a transformed person can trigger processes of transformation in others.

You ask me: "Have you something to say to me?" Remember two things – first, the three rules of ruination. There are three ways to be ruined in this world: first is by sex, second is by gambling, and the third is by politics. Sex is the most fun, gambling is the most exciting, and politics is the surest.

Second, also remember the fundamental law of all revolutions: when the revolution comes, things will be different – not better, just different.

Politicians have been driving the whole world for centuries – to where, to what end? Is it not time enough that we should see the whole stupidity of the game? At least we are aware, fully aware, of five thousand years' of politics; before that the case must have been the same, but after five thousand years of political games what has happened? Man remains in the same darkness, in the same misery, in the same hell. Yes, politics goes on giving him hope – a hope for a better tomorrow, which never comes. Tomorrows never come.

It is the opium of the people. Karl Marx says religion is the opium of the people. It is true, ninety-nine point nine percent it is true; just point one percent it is not true. A Buddha, a Jesus, a Lao Tzu, a Zarathustra – just these few people can be counted in that point one percent, otherwise Karl Marx is ninety-nine point nine percent right, that religion has proved the opium of the people. It has kept people in a drugged state, in such a sleep that they can almost tolerate an intolerable existence, that they can tolerate all kinds of slavery, starvation, in the hope of a better tomorrow. Religions used to give this better tomorrow in the other world, after death.

People come to me and ask, "What will happen after death?" I don't answer them, I ask them another question instead. I ask them, "Forget all about after death, let me ask you one thing: what is happening *before* death?" Because whatever is happening before death will continue to happen after death. It is a continuum: your consciousness will be the same, before or after will not make any difference. The body may not be the same, the container may change, but the content will remain the same. Whatever happens is happening to the content, not to the container.

First, religion was giving opium to the people – "Tomorrow ...

after death." Millions of people remained in that state of druggedness, under that chloroform – religious chloroform. Now politics is doing the same. Even communism has proved nothing but a new opium for the masses – communism is a new kind of religion. The strategy is the same: "Tomorrow the revolution will come and everything will be all right." You have to sacrifice your today for tomorrow, and the tomorrow never comes.

So many years have passed since the Russian Revolution, and tomorrow is still as far away as before. So many years have passed since the Indian Revolution, the Gandhian Revolution, and tomorrow remains as far away, in fact farther away than before. The people who sacrificed, sacrificed in vain; it would have been better if they had lived. The people who were killed were really committing suicide, hoping that they were doing great service to humanity.

Don't create more madness in the world – it is already full of madness.

A colleague of mine once worked in a mental hospital. While making the rounds he would test the patient by asking, "Why are you here?" The response usually revealed the patient's degree of reality orientation.

One morning the psychologist received a response that rocked him. "I am here," replied the patient, "for the same reason you are, doc. I couldn't make a go of it in the outside world."

The patients and the doctors, the people and the politicians are all in the same boat. They are all maniacs! All kinds of maniacs are loose in the world. If you drop out of your radical revolutionary politics, there will be at least one maniac less and that will be a great blessing.

Every structure becomes a prison, and one day or other you have to rebel against it. Have you not observed it down through history? – each revolution in its own turn becomes repressive. In Russia it happened, in China it happened. After every revolution, the revolutionary becomes antirevolutionary. Once he comes into power he has his own structure to impose upon society. And once he starts imposing his structure, slavery changes into a new kind of slavery, but never into freedom.
All revolutions have failed. What I am talking about is not revolution, it is rebellion. Revolution is social, collective; rebellion is individual. We are not interested in giving any structure to society. Enough of structures! Let all structures go. We want individuals in the world – moving freely, moving consciously, of course. And their responsibility comes through their own consciousness. They behave rightly not because they are trying to follow certain commandments; they behave rightly, they behave accurately, because they care.

The Rebel

Can you say more about your notion of rebellion and of a rebel?

My notion about rebellion and the rebel is very simple: a rebel is a man who does not live like a robot conditioned by the past. Religion, society, culture – anything that is of yesterday does not in any way interfere in his way of life, in his style of life.

He lives individually – not as a cog in the wheel, but as an organic unity. His life is not decided by anybody else, but by his own intelligence. The very fragrance of his life is that of freedom. Not only that he lives in freedom, he allows everybody else also to live in freedom. He does not allow anybody to interfere in his life nor does he interfere in anybody else's life. To him, life is so sacred – and freedom is the ultimate value – that he can sacrifice everything for it: respectability, status, even life itself.

Freedom, to him, is what God used to be to the so-called religious people in the past. Freedom is his God.

Men have lived down through the ages like sheep, as part of a crowd, following its traditions, conventions, following the old scriptures and old disciplines. But that way of life was anti-individual; if you are a Christian you cannot be an individual, if you are a Hindu you cannot be an individual.

A rebel is one who lives totally according to his own light, and risks everything else for his ultimate value of freedom.

The rebel is the contemporary person. The mobs are not contemporary. Hindus believe in scriptures which are five or ten thousand years old. Such is also the case with other religions; the dead are dominating the living. The rebel rebels against the dead, takes his life in his own hands. He is not afraid of being alone; on the contrary, he enjoys his aloneness as one of the most precious treasures. The crowd gives you security, safety – at the cost of your soul. It enslaves you. It gives you guidelines on how to live: what to do, what not to do.

All over the world, every religion has given something like the Ten Commandments – and these were given by people who had no idea how the future is going to be, how man's consciousness in the future is going to be. It is as if a small child were to write your whole life's story, not knowing at all what youth means, not knowing at all what old age means, not knowing at all what death is.

All the religions are primitive, crude – and they have been shaping your life. Naturally the whole world is full of misery: you are not allowed to be yourself. Every culture wants you to be just a carbon copy, never your original face.

The rebel is one who lives according to his own light, moves according to his own intelligence. He creates his path by walking on it, he does not follow the crowd on the superhighway. His life is dangerous – but a life that is not dangerous is not life at all. He accepts the challenge of the unknown. He does not meet the unknown that is coming in the future, prepared by the past. That creates the whole anguish of humanity; the past prepares you, and the future is never going to be the past. Your yesterday is never going to be your tomorrow.

But up to now this is how man has lived: your yesterdays prepare you for your tomorrows. The very preparation becomes a hindrance. You cannot breathe freely, you cannot love freely, you cannot dance freely – the past has crippled you in every possible way. The burden of the past is so heavy that everybody is crushed under it. The rebel simply says good-bye to the past.

It is a constant process; hence, to be a rebel means to be continuously in rebellion – because each moment is going to become the past; every day is going to become the past. It is not that the past is already in the graveyard – you are moving through it every moment. Hence, the rebel has to learn a new art: the art of dying to each moment that has passed, so that he can live freely in the new moment that has come.

A rebel is a continuous process of rebellion; he is not static. And that is where I make a distinction between the revolutionary and the rebel.

The revolutionary is also conditioned by the past. He may not be conditioned by Jesus Christ or Gautam Buddha, but he is conditioned by Karl Marx or Mao Zedong or Joseph Stalin or Adolf Hitler or Benito Mussolini. It does not matter who conditions him. The revolutionary has his own holy bible, *Das Kapital*; his holy land, the Soviet Union; his own Mecca, the Kremlin. And just like any other religious person, he is not living according to his own consciousness. He is living according to a conscience created by others. Hence, the revolutionary is nothing but a reactionary. He may be against a certain society, but he is always for another society. He may be against one culture, but he is immediately ready for another culture. He only goes on moving from one prison into another prison – from Christianity to communism. From one religion to another religion – from Hinduism to Christianity. He changes his prisons.

The rebel simply moves out of the past and never allows the past to dominate him. It is a constant, continuous process. The whole life of the rebel is a fire that burns. To the very last breath he is fresh, he is young. He will not respond to any situation according to his past experience; he will respond to every situation according to his present consciousness.

To be a rebel, to me, is the only way to be religious, and the so-called religions are not religions at all. They have destroyed humanity completely, enslaved human beings, chained their souls; so on the surface it seems that you are free, but deep inside you, religions have created a certain conscience which goes on dominating you. A rebel is one who throws away the whole past because he wants to live his own life according to his own longings, according to his own nature – not according to some Gautam Buddha, or according to some Jesus Christ, or Moses.

The rebel is the only hope for the future of humanity.

The rebel will destroy all religions, all nations, all races – because they are all rotten, past, hindering the progress of human evolution. They are not allowing anybody to come to his full flowering: they don't want human beings on the earth – they want sheep.

Jesus continuously says, "I am your shepherd, and you are my sheep..." and I have always wondered that not even a single man stood up and said, "What kind of nonsense are you talking? If we are sheep, then you are also a sheep; and if you are a shepherd, then we are also shepherds." Not only his contemporaries...but for two thousand years no Christian has raised the question that it is such an insult to humanity, such a great humiliation to call human beings sheep and to call himself the shepherd, the savior.

"I have come to save you..." And he could not save himself! Still almost half of humanity is hoping that he will be coming back to save them. You cannot save yourself; the only begotten son of God, Jesus Christ, is needed. He had promised to his people, "I will be coming soon, in your own lifetime" and two thousand years have passed – many lifetimes have passed – and there seems to be no sign, no indication.

But all religions have done the same in different ways. Krishna says in the Gita that whenever there is misery, whenever there is anguish, whenever there is the need, "I will be coming again and again." Five thousand years have passed and he has not been seen even once – never mind "again and again"! These people, however beautiful their statements may be, were not respectful to humanity.

A rebel respects you, respects life, has a deep reverence for everything that grows, thrives, breathes. He does not put himself above you, holier than you, higher than you; he is just one amongst you. Only one thing he can claim: he is more courageous than you are. He cannot save you, only your courage can save you. He cannot lead you, only your own guts can lead you to the fulfillment of your life.

Rebellion is a style of life. To me, it is the only religion which is authentic. Because if you live according to your own light, you may go astray many times and you may fall many times, but each fall, each going astray, will make you wiser, more intelligent, more understanding, more human. There is no other way of learning than by making mistakes. Just don't make the same mistake again. There is no God, except your own consciousness. There is no need for any pope or for any ayatollah or for any *shankaracharya* to be a mediator between you and God. These are the greatest criminals in the world because they are exploiting your helplessness.

Some time ago the pope declared a new sin: that one should not confess directly to God; you have to confess through the priest. Confessing directly to God, communicating directly with God, is a new sin. Strange... You can see clearly that this is not religion, this is business – because if people start confessing directly to God, then who is going to confess to the priest and pay the fine? The priest becomes useless, the pope becomes useless.

All the priests are pretending that they are mediators between you and the ultimate source of life. They know nothing of the ultimate source of life; only you are capable of knowing your source of life. But your source of life is also the ultimate source of life – because we are not separate. No man is an island; we are a vast continent underneath. Perhaps on the surface you look like an island – and there are many islands – but deep down in the ocean you meet. You are part of one earth, one continent. The same is true about consciousness,

But one has to be free from churches, from temples, from mosques, from synagogues. One has to be just oneself and take the challenge of life wherever it leads. You are the only guide. You are your own master.

Existence can be divided into three categories: the known, the unknown, and the unknowable. What is known today was unknown yesterday; what is unknown today may become known tomorrow. So there is not much difference between the known and the unknown. It is only a question of time.

Science, that means the West, believes only in two categories – the known and the unknown. And as a corollary, the scientific mind of the West believes that there will come a day when we will have reduced everything into the known, and there will not be left anything unknown. That is one of the basic assumptions of scientific inquiry. We are everyday discovering more and more; the unknown is shrinking, becoming smaller and the known is becoming bigger.

But if it is true, then that will be the death of humanity. If all is known, then there is no adventure left. Then life will be very empty. If everything is explained, there will not be anything mysterious. And to lose the miraculous, you will lose something tremendously valuable.

It is the unknown, undiscovered, that goes on challenging you to progress, to evolve, to reach new heights, new peaks of consciousness. But if a day comes that all is known, everything is reduced into simple formulas, then there will be no romance, there

will be no poetry, there will be no beauty, there will be no joy. There will be nothing left which is valuable.
The East has a threefold division – known, unknown, unknowable. It agrees with the West that the unknown can become known, but the unknowable will always remain unknowable. There will always be mystery around human consciousness. There will be always mystery around love, friendship, meditation, consciousness. We may be able to know all that is objective, but the subjectivity, the innermost core of human consciousness, will remain always a mystery. And this has been the persistent effort of the East, to make it clear to the whole world that the unknowable should not be denied, otherwise you will take all juice out of human life. You will create robots out of human beings, you will destroy them, and they will be just machines and nothing more.

I heard you say some time ago that science is of the head and religion is of the heart. I understand that these qualities, being of a polarity, are mutually dependent. One cannot exist without the other, just as man cannot exist without both head and heart. Would not then a world scientific community bring with it, as a necessary

> by-product, a world religious community? Is not the vision of a world science and a world religion synthesized in your vision of the New Man?

Man is not only head and heart. There is something more than both in him – his being. So you have to understand three things: the head, the heart, and the being.

I have said religion is of the heart, because religion is the bridge between head and being. The head cannot jump to the being directly unless it goes through the heart.

Science is confined to the head, reason, logic. The heart is confined to feelings, emotions, sensitivities. But the being is beyond both. It is pure silence – no thinking, no feeling. And only the man who knows his being is authentically religious. The heart is only a stopover.

But you have to understand my difficulty. You are in the head. I cannot talk about the being because the head will not be able to communicate with the being. For the head there is no being; that's why scientists go on denying the soul. So I have to talk to you about the heart, which is midway.

It is possible for the head to understand a little bit of the heart because even the greatest scientist falls in love. His head cannot conceive what is happening – falling in love? He cannot prove it rationally, he cannot find why it happened with a particular man or with a particular woman, what the chemistry is behind it, what the physics is behind it; it seems to be something out of nowhere. But he cannot deny it either; it is there, and it is possessing his whole life. That's why I say religion is of the heart. That is only a temporary statement.

Once I can persuade you to move from thinking into feeling, then I can tell you that religion is of the being. Religion is neither thinking nor feeling, it is neither logic nor emotion. It is just pure silence: in one sense utterly empty because there is no feeling, no thinking, and in another sense overflowing with bliss, with benediction.

Meditation is the way from the head to the heart, from the heart to the being.

I would like all the scientists to listen to the heart. That would change the very character of science. It wouldn't be in the service of death, it wouldn't create more and more destructive weapons. It would be in the service of life. It would create better roses, more fragrant roses; it would create better plants, better animals, better birds, better human beings. But the ultimate goal is to move from feeling to being. And if a scientist is capable of using his head as far as the objective world is concerned, using his heart as far as the interpersonal world is concerned, and using his being as far as existence itself is concerned, then he is a perfect man.

My vision of the new man is of a perfect man: perfect in the sense that all his three dimensions are functioning without contradicting each other but, on the contrary, complementing each other.

The perfect man will create a perfect world. The perfect man will create a world of scientists, a world of poets, a world of meditators.

My approach is that all these three centers should be functioning in every person, because even a single individual is a world unto himself. And these centers are in the individual, not in the society; hence, my focus is on the individual. If I can change the individual, sooner or later the world is to follow. It will *have* to follow because it will see the beauty of the new man.

The new man is not only clever in arithmetic, he can also enjoy and compose music. He can dance, he can play the guitar – which is a tremendous relaxation for his head because the head is no longer functioning. And the new man is not only of the heart; there are moments when he drops even deeper and simply is. That source of your is-ness is the very center of your life. To touch it, to be there is to be rejuvenated. All the energies of your heart and of your head will be tremendously multiplied because you will be getting newer energy every day, every moment.

Right now, even a great scientist like Albert Einstein uses only fifteen percent of his potential. What to say about ordinary people? They never go beyond five to seven percent. If all the three centers are functioning together, man will be able to function totally, one hundred percent. We can really create a paradise here, on this earth. It is within our hands. Just a little effort, a little courage, and nothing more is needed.

The world has to be scientific for all the technologies, for all the comforts. The world has to be poetic; otherwise man becomes just a robot. The head is a computer. Without poetry and music and dance and song, what your head does can be done by a computer far more efficiently and infallibly. Popes have been declaring they are infallible. They are not. But if they want to be infallible, their brains can be replaced by a computer; then they will be infallible.

The heart is a totally different dimension – of experiencing beauty, love, and expressing it. But that is not all. Unless you reach your very center you will remain discontented. And a discontented man is dangerous because he will do anything to get rid of his discontentment.

The person who knows himself and his center is the richest. In fact, that's where the kingdom of God is. It is *your* kingdom, there *you* are a god. Deep down, centered in your being, you become an emperor.

A certain mind has come into existence – the American mind. This is something new in the history of humanity. The American mind – and it is for the first time in the whole history of man that such a mind has existed – is the most trained in dealing with the world. American society is the first society in human history which is dominated by the businessman; hence its success. No society has ever been dominated by the businessman. In India it was the scholar, the brahmin, the professor, the pundit, who dominated. In England it was the aristocrats, as it was in the rest of Europe. In Japan it was the warriors, the samurai, who dominated. Never before and nowhere else has the businessman dominated. The American society and culture are based on the mind of the businessman.

The Businessman

I am a businessman. Can I also be a meditator?

One has to do something in life. Somebody is a carpenter and somebody is a king, and somebody is a businessman and somebody is a warrior. These are ways of livelihood, these are ways of getting bread and butter, a shelter. They can't change your inner being. Whether you are a warrior or a businessman does not make any difference: one has chosen one way to earn his livelihood, the other has chosen something else.

Meditation is life, not livelihood.

It has nothing to do with what you *do,* it has everything to do with what you *are.* Yes, business should not enter your being, that is true. If your being also has become businesslike, then it is difficult to meditate and impossible to be a seeker. Because if your being has become businesslike, then you have become too calculative. And a calculative person is a cowardly person: he thinks too much, he cannot take any jumps.

Meditation is a jump: from the head to the heart, and ultimately from the heart to the being. You will be going deeper and deeper, where calculations will have to be left behind, where all logic becomes irrelevant. You cannot carry your cleverness there. In fact, cleverness is not true intelligence either; cleverness is a poor substitute for intelligence. People who are not intelligent learn how to be clever. People who are intelligent need not be clever; they are innocent, they need not be cunning. They function out of a state of not-knowing.

If you are a businessman, that's okay. If Jesus can become a meditator and a seeker, and ultimately a christ, a buddha – and he was the son of a carpenter, helping his father, bringing wood, cutting wood... If a carpenter's son can become a buddha, why not you?

Kabir was a weaver. He continued his work his whole life; even after his enlightenment he was still weaving. He loved it! Many times his disciples asked him, prayed to him with tears in their eyes, "You need not work anymore – we are here to take care of you. So many disciples, why go on spinning, weaving in your old age?"

And Kabir would say, "But do you know for whom I am weaving, for whom I am spinning? For God! – because everyone is now a god to me. It is my way of prayer." If Kabir can become a buddha and still remain a weaver, why can't you?

But business should not enter your being. Business should be just an outside thing, just one of the ways of livelihood. When you close your shop, forget all about your business. When you come home, don't carry the shop in your head. When you are home with your wife, with your children, don't be a businessman. That is ugly: that means your being is becoming colored by your doing. Doing is a superficial thing. The being should remain transcendental to your doing and you should always be capable of putting your doing aside and entering the world of your being. That's what meditation is all about.

So remain a businessman, but for a few hours forget all about it. I am not here to tell you to escape from your ordinary life. I am here to tell you the ways and the means, the alchemy, to transform the ordinary into the extraordinary.

Be a businessman in your shop and don't be a businessman at your home. And sometimes for a few hours forget even the home, the family, the wife, the children. For a few hours just be alone with yourself. Sink deeper and deeper into your own being. Enjoy yourself, love yourself, and slowly, slowly you will become aware that a great joy is welling up, with no cause from the outside world, uncaused from the outside. It is your own flavor, it is your own flowering. This is meditation.

"Sitting silently, doing nothing, the spring comes and the grass grows by itself." Sit silently, doing nothing, and wait for the spring. It comes, it always comes, and when it comes the grass grows by itself. You will see great joy arising in you for no reason at all. Then share it, then give it to people! Then your charity will be inner. Then it will not be just a means to attain some goal; then it will have intrinsic value.

My sannyas is nothing but living in the ordinary world, but living in such a way that you are not possessed by it; remaining transcendental, remaining in the world and yet a little above it. That is sannyas.

It is not the old sannyas in that you have to escape from your wife, your children, your business, and go to the Himalayas. That kind of thing has not worked at all. Many went to the Himalayas but they carried their stupid minds with them. The Himalayas have not been of any help to them; on the contrary, they have destroyed the beauty of the Himalayas, that's all. How can the Himalayas help you? You can leave the world, but you cannot leave your mind here. The mind will go with you; it is inside you. And wherever you are, your same mind will create the same kind of world around you.

You can leave the world – you will be the same. You will again create the same world because you carry the blueprint in your mind. It is not a question of leaving the world, it is a question of changing the mind, renouncing the mind. That's what meditation is.

In America, to be a successful businessman seems to be the ideal. Can you say something about this?

The American mind is the most shallow, ambitious mind that has ever existed in the world. It is the very basic worldly mind. That's why the businessman has become the topmost reality in America. Everything else has faded into the background; the businessman, the man who controls money, is the topmost reality.

Money is the most competitive realm. You need not have culture, you need only have money. You need not know anything about music, anything about poetry. You need not know anything about ancient literature, history, religion, philosophy – no, you need not know. If you have a big bank balance you are important. That's why I say this is the most shallow mind that has ever existed.

And this mind has turned everything into commerce. This mind is continuously in competition. Even if you purchase a Van Gogh or a Picasso, you don't purchase it for Picasso; you purchase because the neighbors have purchased. They have a Picasso in their drawing room, so how can you afford not to have it? You have to have it. You may not know anything, you may not know even how to hang it, which side is which... Because it is difficult to know, as far as a Picasso is concerned, whether the picture is hanging upside-down or right-side up! You may not know at all whether it is authentically a Picasso or not. You may not look at it at all, but because others have it and they are talking about Picasso, you have to show your culture. You simply show your money. So whatever is costly becomes significant, whatever is costly is thought to be significant.

Money and the neighbors seem to be the only criteria to decide everything: their cars, their houses, their paintings, their decorations. People have saunas in their bathrooms not because they love their bodies, not necessarily, but because it is the "in" thing – everybody has it. If you don't have it you look poor. If everybody has a house in the hills you have to have one. You may not know how to enjoy the hills, you may be simply bored there. Or you may take your TV and your radio there and just listen to the same program you were listening to at home, and watch the same TV program as you were watching at home. What difference does it make where you are sitting – in the hills or in your own room? But others have it. A four-car garage is needed; others have it. You may not *need* four cars.

The American mind is continuously competing with others...

Old Luke and his wife were known as the stingiest couple in the valley. Luke died and a few months later his wife lay dying. She called in a neighbor and said weakly, "Ruthie, bury me in my black silk dress. But before you do, cut the back out and make a new dress out of it. It is good material and I hate to waste it."

"Couldn't do that!" exclaims Ruthie. "When you and Luke walk up them golden stairs, what would them angels say if your dress ain't got a back in it?"

"They won't be looking at me," she said. "I buried Luke without his pants."

The concern is always the other – Luke will be without pants so everybody will be looking at him. The American concern is with the other. And the American's life ends when life ends. When the body ends, the American ends; hence, the American is very afraid of death. Because of the fear of death the American goes on trying any way to prolong his life, sometimes to absurd lengths. Now there are many Americans who are just vegetating in hospitals, in mental asylums. They are not living, they are long since dead. They are just managed by the physicians, medicines, modern equipment. Somehow they go on hanging on.

The fear of death is so tremendous: once gone you are gone forever and nothing will survive – because the American knows only the body and nothing else. If you know only the body you are going to be very poor. First, you will always be afraid of death, and one who is afraid to die will be afraid to live – because life and death are so together that if you are afraid to die you will become afraid to live. It is life that brings death, so if you are afraid of death, how can you really love life? The fear will be there. It is life that brings death; you cannot live it totally. If death ends everything, if that is your idea and understanding, then your life will be a life of rushing and chasing. Because death is coming you cannot be patient. Hence the American mania for speed: everything has to be done fast because death is approaching, so try to manage as many more things as possible before you die. Try to stuff your being with as many experiences as possible before you die because once you are dead, you are dead.

This creates a great meaninglessness and, of course, anguish, anxiety. If there is nothing which is going to survive the body, then whatever you do cannot be very deep. Then whatever you do cannot satisfy you. If death is the end and nothing survives, then life cannot have any meaning and significance. Then it is a tale told by an idiot, full of fury and noise, signifying nothing.

So on the one hand the American is constantly running from one place to another to somehow grab the experience, somehow not to miss the experience. He is running all around the world, from one town to another, from one country to another, from one hotel to another. He is running from one guru to another, from one church to another, in search, because death is coming. On the one hand a constant, mad chasing, and on the other hand a deep-down apprehension that everything is useless – because death will end all. So whether you lived a rich life or you lived a poor life, whether you were intelligent or unintelligent, whether you were a great lover or missed, what difference does it make? Finally death comes and it equalizes everybody: the wise and the foolish, the sages and the sinners, the enlightened people and the stupid people, all go down into the earth and disappear. So what is the point of it all? Whether it be a Buddha or a Jesus or a Judas, what difference does it make? Jesus dies on the cross, Judas commits suicide the next day – both disappear into the earth.

On the one hand there is a fear that you may miss and others may attain, and on the other hand a deep apprehension that even if you get what you are after, nothing is had. Even if you arrive, you arrive nowhere because death comes and destroys everything.

The understanding of the mystics of the East is that there is no need to go anywhere. Even if you go on sitting under a tree, as it happened to Buddha... God himself came to him. He was not going anywhere, just sitting under his tree. All comes – you just create the capacity. All comes – you just allow it. Life is ready to happen to you. You are creating so many barriers, and the greatest barrier that you can create is chasing. Because of your chasing and running, whenever life comes and knocks at your door she never finds you there. You are always somewhere else. When life reaches there, you have moved. You were in Katmandu; when life reaches Katmandu you are in Goa. When you are in Goa and life somehow reaches Goa, you are in Pune. And by the time life reaches Pune, you will be in Philadelphia. So, you go on chasing life and life goes on chasing you, and the meeting never happens.

Be. Just be, and wait, and be patient.

The most important thing that happened to the first man who walked on the moon was that he suddenly forgot that he was an American. Suddenly the whole earth was one, there were no boundaries because there is no map on the earth. The American continent, the African continent, the Asian continent, this country and that country all disappeared. Not that he made any effort to put all the opposing camps together; there was not even a Russia or an America, the whole earth was just simply one.

And the first words that were uttered by the American were "My beloved earth!" This is transcendence. For a moment he had forgotten all conditionings: "My beloved earth!" Now the whole earth belonged to him.

This is what actually happens in a state of silence: the whole existence is yours and all opposites disappear into each other, supporting, dancing with each other. It becomes an orchestra.

The scene was the latest Olympic games. In the quarters of the American wrestling team stood John Mack, the trainer, warning his protégé, Mike "Bull" Flamm, about the forthcoming match.

"You know," Mack said, "the Georgian wrestler you are about to tackle, Ivan Katruvsky, is one of the greatest wrestlers in the world. But he really is not as good as you are. The only thing he's got that makes him a terror is his pretzel-hold. If he once gets a man in his pretzel-hold, that man is doomed. He has used the pretzel-hold on twenty-seven competitors and in each case his opponent gave up within ten seconds.

"So, listen to me, Bull, you have got to be damned careful. Never let him get you in that pretzel-hold. If he once clamps you in it, you're a goner!"

Bull listened carefully to Mack's instructions on how to avoid that crippling grip of Ivan's. For the first three minutes of the bout, neither the American nor the Georgian could gain an advantage. The crowd was on edge. Then, suddenly, pandemonium broke loose – Bull Flamm had fallen into the clutches of Ivan's pretzel-hold and was moaning in agony. Mack knew the match was lost and he left the arena in deep gloom. Down the corridor, the echoes of Bull's anguished cries still reached him. And then, as Mack was about to enter his quarters, he heard an enormous shout arise from the stadium, a cheer the likes of which he had never heard in all his long experience. The stands were in absolute uproar. From the shouts, Mack knew that Bull had won the match, but he couldn't understand it. What could have caused the unthinkable turnabout?

A minute later Flamm came trotting into the American dressing room. His trainer threw his arms around him, and said, "Bull, how in hell did you ever get out of that pretzel-hold?"

"Well," answered Flamm, "he twisted me into such shapes that I never felt such agony in my life. I thought my bones were going to break. And as I was just about to faint I saw two balls hanging in front of me. With one desperate lunge, I bit those balls. Well, Mack, you can't imagine what a man is capable of when he bites his own balls."

You must have heard about the Japanese discipline of karate. The word karate *is very meaningful. It comes from a root which means empty-hand. It says: a man can become a great warrior if he understands totally the meaning of being empty. If somebody understands that "Empty-handed I have come, empty-handed I will go, and empty-handed I am here," then there is nothing to lose. Who can conquer a person who has nothing to lose? Who can defeat a person who has nothing to lose? Who can frighten a person who has nothing to lose? By understanding this emptiness he becomes a great warrior. It is impossible to defeat him, it is impossible to rob him, it is impossible to kill him – because he is already empty. He holds nothing in his hands. By not holding anything, he goes beyond life and death.*

The Warrior

Being a businessman and a professional, how can I be a warrior at the same time? Am I going to miss enlightenment?

To be a warrior doesn't mean to be a soldier, it is a quality of the mind. You can be a businessman and be a warrior; you can be a warrior and be a businessman.

"Businessman" means a quality of the mind which is always bargaining, trying to give less and get more. That's what I mean when I say "businessman" : trying to give less and get more, always bargaining, always thinking about profit. A warrior is again a quality of the mind, the quality of the gambler, not of the bargainer, the quality which can stake everything this way or that – a non-compromising mind.

If a businessman thinks of enlightenment, he thinks of it as a commodity like many other commodities. He has a list: he has to make a big palace, he has to purchase this and that, and in the end he has to purchase enlightenment also. But enlightenment is always the last: when everything is done, then; when nothing remains to be done, then. And that enlightenment is also to be purchased because he understands only money.

It happened that a great and rich man came to Mahavira. He was really very rich; he could purchase anything, even kingdoms. Even kings borrowed money from him.

He came to Mahavira and he said, "I have been hearing so much about meditation, and during the time you have been here you have created a craze in people; everybody is talking about meditation.

What *is* meditation? How much does it cost and can I purchase it?"

Mahavira hesitated, so the man said, "Don't think about the cost at all. Simply say and I will pay; there is no problem about it."

How to talk to this man? – Mahavira was at a loss as to what to say to him. Finally Mahavira said, "Go... In your town there is a man, a very poor man; he may be willing to sell his meditation. He has achieved it, and he is so poor that he may be ready to sell it."

The man thanked Mahavira, rushed to the poor man, knocked on his door and said, "How much do you want for your meditation? I want to purchase your meditation."

The man started laughing. He said, "You can purchase *me*, that's okay. But how can I give you my meditation? It is a quality of my being, it is not a commodity."

But businessmen have always been thinking in this way. They donate to purchase something, they create temples to purchase something. They give, but their giving is never a giving; it is always to get something, it is an investment.

When I say to you to be a warrior, I mean to be a gambler, to put everything at stake. Then enlightenment becomes a question of life and death, not a commodity, and you are ready to throw away everything for it. And you are not thinking about the profit.

People come to me and they ask, "What will we gain out of meditation? What is the purpose of it? What will be the profit out of it? If one hour is devoted to meditation, what will be the gain?" Their whole life is economy.

A warrior is not after gain; a warrior is after a peak, a peak of experiencing. What does a warrior gain when he fights in a war? Your soldiers are not warriors any longer, they are just servants. Warriors are no longer on this earth because the whole thing is being done by technology. You drop a bomb on Hiroshima; the dropper is not a warrior. Any child can do that, any madman can do that – really, only a madman can do it. Dropping a bomb on Hiroshima is not being a fighter or a warrior.

War is no longer the same as it was in the past; now anybody can do it, and sooner or later only mechanical devices will do it. A plane without a pilot can do it – and the plane is not a warrior. The quality is lost.

The warrior was facing, encountering, the enemy, face-to-face. Just imagine two people with drawn swords encountering each other: Can they think? If they think they will miss. Thinking stops; when swords are drawn, thinking stops. They cannot plan because if they plan, in that moment, the other will hit. They move spontaneously, they become no-minds. The danger is so much, the possibility of death is so near, that the mind cannot be allowed to function. The mind needs time; in emergencies the mind cannot be allowed. When you are sitting in your chair you can think, but when you are facing an enemy you cannot think.

If you pass along a street, a dark street, and suddenly you see a snake, a dangerous snake sitting there, what will you do? Will you start thinking? No, you will jump. And this jump will not be out of your mind because the mind needs time, and snakes don't have any time; they don't have any mind. The snake will strike you – so the mind cannot be allowed. While facing a snake you jump, and that jump comes out of your being; it comes before thought. You jump first and then you think.

This is what I mean by the quality of a warrior: action comes without thinking, action is without mind; action is total. You can become a warrior without going to war, there is no need to go to war.

The whole of life is an emergency and everywhere there are enemies and snakes, and ferocious wild animals ready to attack you. The whole of life is a war. If you are alert you will see that the whole of life is a war, and any moment you can die; so the emergency is permanent. Be alert, be like a warrior as if moving amidst the enemy. Any moment, from anywhere, death can jump on you; don't allow the mind. And be a gambler – only gamblers can take this jump. The jump is so much that those who think of profit cannot take it. It is a risk, the greatest risk; you may be lost and nothing may be gained. When you come to me you may lose everything and you may not gain anything.

I will repeat one of Jesus' sayings: "Whosoever clings to life, whosoever tries to preserve it, will lose it; and whosoever is ready to lose it will preserve it." This is talking in the language of a gambler: lose it – this is the way to preserve it. Die – that is the way to reach eternal life, immortal life.

When I say a businessman, I say a calculating, cunning mind. Don't be cunning minds. No child is ever a businessman, and it is difficult to find an old man who is not a businessmen. Every child is a warrior and every old man is a businessman. How every warrior becomes a businessman is a long story: the whole society, education, culture, conditioning, makes you more and more fearful, afraid. You cannot take a risk, and everything that is beautiful *is* risky.

Love is a risk. Life is a risk. God is a risk. God is the greatest risk, and through mathematics you will not reach; only through taking the ultimate risk, putting everything that you have at stake. And you don't know the unknown; the known you risk and the unknown you don't know.

The business mind will say, "What are you doing – losing that which you have for that which no one knows exists or not? Preserve that which is in hand and don't long for the unknown." The warrior mind says, "The known has been known already, now there is nothing in it; it has become a burden and to carry it is useless. The unknown must be known now, and I must risk the known for the unknown."

And if you can risk, totally risk, not preserving anything, not playing tricks with yourself, not withholding anything, suddenly the unknown envelops you. And when it comes, you become aware that it is not only the unknown, it is the unknowable. It is not against the known, it is beyond the known. To move in that darkness, to move in that uncharted place without any maps and without any pathways, to move alone into that absolute, the quality of the warrior is needed.

Many of you still have a little of it left because you were once children; you were all warriors, you were all dreamers of the unknown. That childhood is hidden but it cannot be destroyed; it is there, it still has its own corner in your being. Allow it to function; be childlike and you will be warriors again. That's what I mean.

And don't feel depressed because you run a shop and you are a businessman. Don't feel depressed; you can be a warrior anywhere. To take risks is a quality of the mind, a childlike quality – to trust and to move beyond that which is secure.

The greatest warrior has nothing to do with war. He has nothing to do with fighting others. He has something to do inside himself. And it is not a fight, although it brings victory; it is not a war, not a conflict. But one has to be a warrior because one has to be very alert just like a warrior.

One has to be very watchful, very meditative, because if one is moving in the darkest continent in existence... Ultimately there is light, infinite light, but first one has to pass through a great dark night of the soul. There are all kinds of pitfalls, all possibilities of going astray and there are all kinds of inner enemies. They have not to be killed or destroyed; they have to be transformed, they have to be converted into friends. Anger has to be transformed into compassion, lust has to be transformed into love, and so on, so forth. So it is not a war, but certainly one needs to be a warrior.

That's how, in Japan, the whole world of the samurai, the warrior, came out of meditation and all kinds of martial arts became paths toward inner peace. Swordsmanship became one of the most meditative things in Japan. One has to be very alert because a single moment of unconsciousness, and you are finished.

The real swordsman becomes so alert that before the other person attacks him he knows. Before the thought of attack has even crossed the other's mind, he has prepared himself. He is ready. His watchfulness becomes so deep that he starts reading the thoughts of the other. It is said that if two real samurais fight nobody can win. The fight can continue but nobody can win because both will be reading the other's mind. And before you can attack, the other is already there to defend.

Swordsmanship became one of the greatest sources of enlightenment. It seems strange, but Japan has done many really strange things. From tea drinking to swordsmanship, everything has been changed into meditation. In fact the whole of life can be transformed into meditation, because meditation simply means becoming more aware.

So go inward and be more aware. One day victory is yours – that is absolutely certain. You just have to fulfil the requirement: you have to be totally aware.

~

It happened once, a Zen samurai, a Zen warrior, had come home early from the front and he found his servant making love to his wife. Being a man of Zen, he said to the servant, "Don't be worried, just finish your job. I am waiting outside. You will have to take a sword in your hand and fight with me. It is perfectly okay whatever is happening. I am waiting outside."

This poor servant started trembling. He does not even know how to hold a sword, and his master is a famous warrior: he will chop off his head in a single blow. So he ran out from the back door to the Zen master who was also the warrior's master. He said to the master, "I have got into trouble. It is all my fault, but it has happened."

The master listened to his story and he said, "There is no need to be worried. I will teach you how to hold the sword, and I will also tell you that it does not matter that your master is a great warrior. All that matters is spontaneity. And in spontaneity you will be the better because he seems to be confident: "There is no question of this servant surviving. It will be almost like a cat playing with a rat." So don't be worried. Be total and hit him hard because this is your only chance of living, survival. So don't be halfhearted, don't be conditional, thinking that perhaps he may forgive you. He will never forgive you – you will have to fight with him. You have provoked and challenged him. But there is no problem: as far as I can see, you will end up the winner."

The servant could not believe it and the master said, "You should understand that I am his master also, and I know that he will behave according to his training. Knowing perfectly well that he is going to win, he cannot be unconditional – and you have no other alternative than to be unconditional. Just be total. You don't know where to hit, how to hit, so hit anywhere. Just go crazy!"

The servant said, "If you say so, I will do it. In fact there is no chance of my survival, so why not do it totally!"

Seeing that the time had come, he learned how to hold the sword, and he came back and challenged his master, "Now come on!"

The samurai could not believe it. He was thinking the servant would fall at his feet and cry and weep and say, "Just forgive me!" But instead of that the servant roared like a lion, and he had got a sword from the Zen master! The samurai recognized the sword and he asked, "From where did you get it?"

The servant said, "From your master. Now come, let it be decided once and for all. Either I will survive or you will survive, but both cannot." The samurai felt a little tremble in his heart, but still he thought, "How can he manage? It is years' training... I have been fighting for years in wars, and this poor servant..." But he had to take out his sword.

The servant went really crazy. Not knowing where to hit, he was hitting here and there and just... The samurai was at a loss because he could fight with any warrior who knew how to fight – but this man knew nothing and he was doing all kinds of things! The servant pushed him to the wall and the samurai had to ask him, "Please forgive me. You will kill me. You don't know how to fight – what are you doing?"

The servant said, "It is not a question of doing. It is my last moment; I will do everything with totality."

The servant was the winner and the warrior went to the master and said, "What miracle have you done? Within five minutes he became such a great warrior, and he was making such blows, so stupid that he could have killed me. He knows nothing but he could have killed me. He pushed me to the wall of my house, his sword on my chest. I had to ask to be forgiven and tell him that whatever he is doing it is perfectly okay and to continue."

The master said, "You have to learn a lesson, that it is finally the totality, the unconditional absoluteness... Whether it brings defeat or victory does not matter. What matters is that the man was total, and the total man never is defeated. His totality is his victory."

If one keeps growing up in maturity and understanding, one never becomes old; one is always young because one is always learning. Learning keeps you young. One is always young because one is not burdened with repressions. And because one is weightless, one feels as if one is just a child – a newcomer to this beautiful earth. Risk everything to be natural and you will not be at a loss.

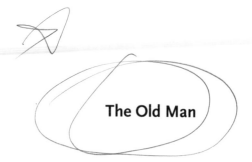

The Old Man

Why is there such an expression as "dirty old man"? I am getting old and I suspect people are beginning to think about me in exactly those words.

It is because of a long, long repressive society that the dirty old man exists. It is because of your saints, your priests, your puritans, that the old dirty man exists.

If people are allowed to live their sexual life joyously, by the time they are nearing forty-two – remember, I am saying forty-two, not eighty-four – just when they are nearing forty-two, sex will start losing its grip on them. Just as sex arises and becomes very powerful by the time one is fourteen, in exactly the same way by the time one is forty-two it starts disappearing. It is a natural course. And when sex disappears, the old man has a love, has compassion, of a totally different kind. There is no lust in his love, no desire, he wants to get nothing out of it. His love has a purity, an innocence; his love is a joy.

Sex gives you pleasure. And sex gives you pleasure only when you have gone into sex; then pleasure is the end result. If sex has become irrelevant – not repressed, but because you experienced it so deeply that it is no longer of any value... You have known it, and knowledge always brings freedom. You have known it totally and because you have known it, the mystery is finished, there is nothing more to explore. In that knowing, the whole energy, the sexual energy, is transmuted into love, compassion. Then one gives out of joy. Then the old man is the most beautiful man in the world, the cleanest man in the world.

There is no such expression in any language as the "clean old man." I have never heard it. But this expression, the "dirty old man," exists in almost all languages. The reason is that the body becomes old, the body becomes tired, the body wants to get rid of all sexuality – but the mind still hankers because of repressed desires. When the body is not capable, and the mind continuously haunts you for something which the body is incapable of doing, really the old man is in a mess. His eyes are sexual, lusty; his body dead and dull. And his mind goes on goading him. He starts having a dirty look, a dirty face; he starts having something ugly in him.

It reminds me of the story of the man who overheard his wife and her sister discussing his frequent out-of-town business trips. The sister kept suggesting that the wife should worry about her husband being unchaperoned at those posh resort convention hotels with so many attractive, unattached career women around.

"Me worry?" said the wife. "Why, he'd never cheat on me. He's too loyal, too decent, too old..."

The body sooner or later becomes old – it is bound to become old – but if you have not lived your desires they will clamor around you, they are bound to create something ugly in you. Either the old man becomes the most beautiful man in the world, because he attains an innocence the same as the innocence of a child, or even far deeper than the innocence of a child – he becomes a sage. But if desires are still there, running like an undercurrent, then he is caught in a turmoil.

A very old man was arrested while attempting to sexually molest a young woman. Seeing such an old man, eighty-four, in court, the magistrate reduced the charge from rape to assault with a dead weapon.

If you are becoming old, remember that old age is the climax of life. Remember that old age can be the most beautiful experience – because the child has hopes for the future, he lives in the future. He has great desires to do this, to do that. Every child thinks that he is going to be somebody special – Alexander the Great, Josef Stalin, Mao Zedong. He lives in desires and in the future. The young man is too possessed by the instincts, all the instincts, exploding in him. Sex is there: the young man is possessed by such great natural forces that he cannot be free. Ambition is there, and time is running out fast, and he has to do something and he has to be something. All those hopes and desires and fantasies of childhood have to be fulfilled; he is in a great rush, in a hurry.

The old man knows that those childish desires were really childish. The old man knows that all those days of youth and turmoil are gone. The old man is in the same state as when a storm has gone and silence prevails. That silence can be of tremendous beauty, depth, richness. If the old man is really mature, which is very rarely the case, then he will be beautiful. But people only grow in age, they don't grow up. Hence the problem.

Grow up, become more mature, become more alert and aware. And old age is the last opportunity given to you: before death comes, prepare. And how does one prepare for death? By becoming more meditative.

If some lurking desires are still there, and the body is getting old and the body is not capable of fulfilling those desires, don't be worried. Meditate over those desires, watch, be aware. Just by being aware and watchful and alert, those desires and the energy contained in them can be transmuted. But before death comes, be free of all desires.

When I say be free of all desires I simply mean be free of all objects of desire. Then there is a pure longing. That pure longing is divine, that pure longing is God. Then there is pure creativity with no object, with no address, with no direction, with no destination – just pure energy, a pool of energy, going nowhere. That's what buddhahood is.

~

Except man, in the whole of existence nobody suffers from old age; in fact, existence knows nothing about old age. It knows about ripening; it knows about maturing. It knows that there is a time to dance, to live as intensely and as totally as possible, and there is a time to rest.

Those old leaves of the almond tree by the side of my house are not dying; they are simply going to rest, melting and merging into the same earth from which they have arisen. There is no sadness, no mourning, but an immense peace in falling to rest in eternity. Perhaps another day, another time they may be back again, in some other form, on some other tree. They will dance again; they will sing again; they will rejoice the moment.

Existence knows only a circular change from birth to death, from death to birth, and it is an eternal process. Every birth implies death and every death implies birth. Every birth is preceded by a death and every death is succeeded by a birth. Hence existence is not afraid. There is no fear anywhere except in the mind of man.

Man seems to be the only sick species in the whole cosmos. Where is this sickness? It should really have been otherwise: man should have enjoyed more, loved more, lived more each moment. Whether the moment is of childhood or of youth or of old age, whether it is of birth or of death, does not matter at all. You are transcendental to all these small episodes.

Thousands of births have happened to you, and thousands of deaths. And those who can see clearly can understand it even more deeply, as if this is happening every moment. Something in you dies every moment and something in you is born anew. Life and death are not so separate, not separated by seventy years.

Life and death are just like two wings of a bird, simultaneously happening. Neither life can exist without death, nor death exist without life. Obviously they are not opposites; obviously they are complementaries. They need each other for their existence; they are interdependent. They are part of one cosmic whole.

But because man is so unaware, so asleep, he is incapable of seeing a simple and obvious fact. Just a little awareness, not much, and you can see you are changing every moment. And change means something is dying, something is being reborn. Then birth and death become one; then childhood and its innocence become one with old age and its innocence.

There is a difference, yet there is no opposition. The child's innocence is really poor because it is almost synonymous with ignorance. The old man, ripe in age, who has passed through all the experiences of darkness and light, of love and hate, of joy and misery, who has been matured through life in different situations, has come to a point where he is no longer a participant in any experience. Misery comes and he watches. Happiness comes and he watches. He has become a watcher on the hill. Everything passes down in the dark valleys, but he remains on the sunlit peak of the mountain, simply watching in utter silence.

The innocence of old age is rich. It is rich from experience; it is rich from failures, from successes; it is rich from right actions, from wrong actions; it is rich from all the failures, from all the successes; it is rich multidimensionally. Its innocence cannot be synonymous with ignorance. Its innocence can only be synonymous with wisdom.

Both the child and the old man are innocent. But their innocences have a qualitative change, a qualitative difference. The child is innocent because he has not yet entered the dark night of the soul; the old man is innocent – he has come out of the tunnel. One is entering the tunnel; the other is getting out of the tunnel. One is going to suffer much; one has already suffered enough. One cannot avoid the hell that is ahead of him; the other has left the hell behind him.

Your question is the question of almost every human being. Knowingly or unknowingly there is a trembling in the heart that you are becoming old, that after old age the deluge – after old age, death. And for centuries you have been made so afraid of death that the very idea has become deep-rooted in your unconscious; it has gone deep in your blood, in your bones, in your marrow. The very word frightens you – not that you know what death is, but just because of thousands of years of conditioning that death is the end of your life, you are afraid.

I want you to be absolutely aware that death is not the end. In existence, nothing begins and nothing ends. Just look all around: the evening is not the end, nor is the morning the beginning. The morning is moving toward the evening and the evening is moving toward the morning. Everything is simply moving into different forms. There is no beginning and there is no end.

Why should it be otherwise with man? Man is not an exception. In this idea of being exceptional, in being more special than the other animals and the trees and the birds, man has created his own hell, his paranoia. The idea that we are exceptional beings, we are human beings, has created a rift between you and existence. That rift causes all your fears and your misery, causes unnecessary anguish and angst in you.

And all your so-called leaders, whether religious or political or social, have emphasized the rift; they have widened it. There has not been a single effort in the whole history of man to bridge the rift, to bring man back to the earth, to bring man back with the animals and with the birds and with the trees, and to declare an absolute unity with existence.

That is the truth of our being. Once it is understood, you are neither worried about old age nor worried about death because looking around you, you can be absolutely satisfied that nothing ever begins, it has always been there; nothing ever ends, it will always remain there.

The idea of being old fills you with great anxiety. It means now your days of life, of love, of rejoicings are over; now you will exist only in name. It will not be a rejoicing, but only a dragging toward the grave. Obviously you cannot enjoy the idea that you are just a burden in existence, just standing in a queue which is moving every moment toward the graveyard.

It is one of the greatest failures of all cultures and all civilizations in the world that they have not been able to provide a meaningful life, a creative existence for their old; that they have not been able to provide a subtle beauty and grace, not only to old age, but to death itself.

And the problem becomes more complicated because the more you are afraid of death, the more you will be afraid of life too. Each moment lived, death comes closer. A man who is afraid of death cannot be in love with life, because it is life finally that takes you to the doors of death. How can you love life? It was for this reason that all the religions started renouncing life: renounce life because that is the only way to renounce death. If you don't live life, if you are already finished with the job of living, loving, dancing, singing, then naturally you need not be afraid of death; you have died already.

We have called these dead people saints; we have worshipped them. We have worshipped them because we knew we would also like to be like them, although we don't have that much courage. At least we can worship and show our intentions. If we had courage, or if one day we gather courage, we would also like to live like them: utterly dead. The saint cannot die because he has already died. He has renounced all the pleasures, all the joys; all that life offers he has rejected. He has returned the ticket to existence saying, "I am no longer part of the show." He has closed his eyes.

It happened once that a so-called saint was visiting me. I took him into the garden – there were so many beautiful dahlias, and I showed him those beautiful flowers in the morning sun. He looked very strangely at me, a little annoyed, irritated, and he could not resist the temptation to condemn me, saying, "I thought you were a religious person – and you are still enjoying the beauty of the flowers?"

On one point he is right, that if you are enjoying the beauty of the flowers, you cannot avoid enjoying the beauty of human beings; you cannot avoid enjoying the beauty of women; you cannot avoid enjoying the beauty of music and dance. If you are interested in the beauty of the flowers, you have shown that you are still interested in life, that you cannot yet renounce love. If you are aware of beauty, how can you avoid love? Beauty provokes love; love imparts beauty.

I said, "On this point you are right, but on the second point you are wrong. Whoever told you that I am a religious person? I am not yet dead! To be religious the basic requirement is to be dead. If you are alive you can only be a hypocrite, you cannot be really religious."

When you see a bird on the wing, it is impossible not to rejoice in its freedom. And when you see the sunset with all the colors spread on the horizon – even if you close your eyes, your very effort of closing the eyes will show your interest. You have been overwhelmed by the beauty of it.

Life is another name of love. And love is nothing but being sensitive to beauty.

I said to that so-called saint, "I can renounce religion, but I cannot renounce life because life has been given to me by existence itself, and religion is just man-made, manufactured by the priests and the politicians; manufactured to deprive man of his joy, to deprive man of his dignity, to deprive man of his humanity itself.

"I am not a religious person in your sense. I have a totally different definition of being religious. To me the religious person is one who is totally alive, intensely alive, aflame with love, aware of tremendous beauty all around; has the courage to rejoice each moment of life and death together. Only a man who is so capable of rejoicing in life and death – only his song continues. It does not matter whether life is happening or death is happening, his song is not disturbed, his dance does not waver."

Only such an adventurous soul, only such a pilgrim of existence is religious. But in the name of religion man has been given poor substitutes, false, phony, meaningless, just toys to play with. Worshipping statues, chanting man-made mantras, paying tributes to those who have been cowards and escapists and who were not able to live life because they were so afraid of death, and calling them saints, religion has distracted man from true and authentic religiousness.

You need not be worried about old age. And it is even more beautiful that people have starting thinking about you as ancient. That means you have attained the real transcendence, you have lived everything. Now it is your maturity. You have not renounced anything, but you have simply passed through every experience. You have grown so experienced that now you need not repeat those experiences again and again. This is transcendence.

You should rejoice, and I would like the whole world to understand the rejoicing that is our birthright in accepting with deep gratitude old age and the final consummation of old age in death.

If you are not graceful about it, if you cannot laugh at it, if you cannot disappear into the eternal leaving laughter behind, you have not lived rightly. You have been dominated and directed by wrong people. They may have been your prophets, your messiahs, your saviors, your *tirthankaras*; they may have been your incarnations of gods, but they have all been criminals in the sense that they have deprived you of life and they have filled your hearts with fear.

My effort here is to fill your heart with laughter. Your every fiber of being should love to dance in every situation, whether it is day or night, whether you are down or up. Irrespective of the situation, an undercurrent of cheerfulness should continue. That is authentic religiousness to me.

Part 4

THE NEW MAN

The idea of a better man is an old idea, very old, as old as man himself. Everybody is willing to accept a better man because it needs no radical change. A better man means something is added to you: you remain the same, you remain continuous; there is no discontinuity. And you become richer, better. The idea of a better man is rooted in greed, hence everybody will support it.

To talk about the new man is dangerous. A new man means cutting away totally from the past, disrupting, uprooting yourself completely from the past, dying to the past and living in the present. And old habits die very hard. We have become accustomed to hearing about a better man; it has gone into the very circulation of our blood. Every saint, every mahatma talks about the better man; that's his business, we know. But about a new man? Then we become afraid. He is bringing something absolutely new; he is taking us into the territory of the unknown, he is trying to uproot us from the familiar. And we have lived for thousands of years in a particular way; we are conditioned by it, we are part of it. Only very few people can manage to get out of it. Hence my message is going to remain only for the chosen few.

Remember, old habits die hard – and our religions, our philosophies are very old, our styles of life are very old. And I am for the new. We think the old is

The New Man

gold – and I say the old is just junk! I agree with Henry Ford that history is bunk. It is all bullshit! We have to free man from all that has gone before, and we have to free man totally, absolutely, categorically.

What according to you is the most significant thing that is happening today in the world?

A new man is emerging. The image of the new man is not yet clear, but the horizon is becoming red and the sun will soon be there. The morning mist is there and the image of the new man is vague, but still, a few things are very crystal clear about the new man.

And this is of tremendous importance because since monkeys became man, man has remained the same. A great revolution is on the way. It will be far more deep-going than the revolution that happened when monkeys started walking on the earth and became human beings. That change created the mind, that change brought psychology in. Now another far more significant change is going to happen that will bring the soul in, and man will not only be a psychological being but a spiritual being too.

You are living in one of the most alive times ever. The new man, in fragments, has already arrived, but only in fragments. And the new man has been arriving for centuries, but only here and there. That's how things happen: when the spring comes it starts with one flower. But when one flower is there, one can be certain the spring is not far away – it has come. The first flower has heralded its coming. Zarathustra, Krishna, Lao Tzu, Buddha, Jesus – these were the first flowers. Now, on a greater scale, the new man is going to be born.

This new consciousness is the most important thing that is happening today, according to me. I would like to tell you something about this new consciousness – its orientations, and its characteristics – because you are to help it to come out of the womb, because you have to be it. The new man cannot come from nowhere, it has to come through you. The new man can only be born through your womb: you have to become the womb.

Sannyas is an experimentation: to clean the ground so that new seeds can fall in. If you understand the meaning of the new man, you will be able to understand the significance of sannyas too. And it is because sannyas is concerned with the new man that the old orthodoxies of all kinds are going to be against me and against sannyas – because this is their end. If sannyas succeeds, if the new man succeeds, the old will have to go. The old can live only if the new man is prevented from coming.

It cannot be prevented now because it is not only a question of the new man's coming into existence. It is a question of the survival of the whole earth – of consciousness itself, of life itself. It is a question of life and death. The old man has come to utter destructiveness. The old man has reached the end of its tether. Now there is no life possible with the old concept of man, but only death. The old man is preparing for a global suicide. The old man is piling up atom bombs, hydrogen bombs, in order to commit a collective suicide. This is a very unconscious desire: rather than allowing the new man to be, the old man would like to destroy the whole thing.

You have to understand, you have to protect the new, because the new carries the whole future with it. And man has come to a stage where a great quantum leap is possible.

The old man was otherworldly, the old man was against this world. The old man was always looking to the heavens. The old man was more concerned with life after death than life before death. The new man's concern will be life before death. The new man's concern will be this life, because if this life is taken care of, the other will follow on its own accord. One need not worry about it, one need not think about it.

The old man was too concerned with God. That concern was out of fear. The new man will not be concerned with God, but will live and love this world, and out of that love will experience the existence of God. The old man was speculative, the new man is going to be existential.

The old man can be defined in the Upanishadic statement: *neti neti*, not this, not this. The old man was negative – life-negative, life-denying. The new man will be life-affirming: *iti iti*, this and this. The old man's concern was that, the new man's concern will be this, because out of this, that is born, and if you become too concerned with that, you miss both.

Tomorrow is in the womb of today: take care of today and you have taken care of tomorrow. There is no need to be worried in any way about tomorrow. And if you become too worried about tomorrow you have missed today! Tomorrow will come as today – it always comes as today. And if you have learned this suicidal habit of missing today, you will miss tomorrow also. You will go on missing.

The old man was continuously missing, was miserable, sad. And because he was sad he was against the world, he blamed the world, he blamed samsara. He said, "It is because of the world that I am in misery." It is not so. The world is immensely beautiful – it is all beauty, bliss, and benediction. There is nothing wrong with the world. Something was wrong with the old mind. The old mind was either past-oriented or future-oriented – which are not really different orientations. The old mind was concerned with that which is not.

The new man will be utterly in tune with that which is, because that is God, that is reality: *iti iti*, this is it. This moment has to be lived in its totality. This moment has to be lived in its spontaneity, with no a priori ideas. The old man was carrying ready-made answers. He was stuffed with philosophy, religion, and all kinds of nonsense.

The new man is going to live life without any a priori conclusion about it. Without any conclusion, one has to face existence and then one knows what it is. If you have already concluded, your conclusion will become a barrier, it will not allow you inquiry. Your conclusion will become a blindfold, it will not allow you to see the truth. Your investment will be in the conclusion, you will distort reality to fit your conclusion. That's what has been done up to now.

The new man will not be Hindu, will not be Mohammedan, will not be Christian, will not be communist. The new man will not know all these "isms." The new man will be simply an opening, a window to reality. He will allow reality as it is. He will not project his own mind upon it, he will not use reality as a screen. His eyes will be available, they will not be full of ideas.

The new man will not live out of belief, he will simply live. And remember, only those who can simply live without belief come to know what truth is. The believer or the disbeliever never come to know what truth is – their beliefs are too heavy on their minds, they are surrounded too much by their belief systems. The new man will not know any belief system. He will watch, he will observe, he will see, he will live, and he will allow all kinds of experiences. He will be available, he will be multidimensional. He will not carry scriptures in his head, he will carry only alertness, awareness. He will be meditative.

The old man lived out of fear – even his God was nothing but a creation out of fear. His temples, mosques, *gurudwaras*, churches – they were all out of fear. He was trembling, he was afraid. The new man will live out of love, not out of fear, because fear serves death, love serves life. And if you live out of fear you will never know what life is, you will only know death, again and again.

And remember, the person who lives out of fear creates all kinds of situations in which he has to feel more and more fear. Your fear creates situations, just as your love creates situations: if you love you will find so many occasions to be loving, if you are afraid you will find so many occasions to be afraid. Love is going to be the taste of the new consciousness.

Because fear was the taste of the old consciousness it created wars. In three thousand years, man has fought five thousand wars – as if we have not been doing anything else, continuous fighting somewhere or other. This is a very mad state of affairs, humanity's past is insane.

The new man will become discontinuous with this insane past. He will believe in love, not in war. He will believe in life, not in death. He will be creative, not destructive. His science, his art – all will serve creativity. He will not create bombs. He will not be political because politics is out of hatred. Politics is rooted in fear, hate, destructiveness. The new man will not be political, the new man will not be national. The new man will be global. He will not have any political ambition because it is stupid to have political ambition. The new man is going to be very intelligent. The first signs of that intelligence are rising on the horizon. Those who have eyes can see it: the children are rebelling.

It is a great moment of rejoicing that the young people all over the world are rebelling against all kinds of orthodoxies – whether the orthodoxy is that of church or state doesn't matter. They are not ready to obey – not that they have determined to disobey, they are not determined to disobey either. They will meditate, and if they feel like obeying they will obey, if they feel like disobeying they will disobey. They have no fixed ideology. "My country right or wrong" – they cannot make such stupid statements. Sometimes it is wrong, sometimes it is right. When it is right, the new man will support it, when it is wrong whether it is one's own country or not doesn't matter. It may be one's own family – one's own father, mother – but if it is wrong, it is wrong.

The new man will live not out of prejudices but out of spontaneous responsibility. The old man was a slave, the new man will be free. The new man will have freedom at the very core of his being.

The old man was very serious, the old man was a workaholic. The new man will be playful – *homo ludens*. He will believe in enjoying life. He will drop words like *duty*, *sacrifice*. He will not sacrifice for anything. He will not be a victim to any altar – that of the state or of the religion, of the priest or of the politician. He will not allow anybody to exploit his life: "Go and die because your country is at war." His commitment is toward life, his commitment is not toward anything else. He wants to live in joy, he wants to rejoice in all the gifts of God, he wants to celebrate. Alleluia will be his only mantra.

Jesus says, "Rejoice, rejoice. I say unto you rejoice." Man has not rejoiced yet. Man has lived under a great burden of seriousness. Work for the country, work for the family, work for the wife, work for the children, work for your father and mother – just go on working and working and then one day die and disappear into the grave. And then others will work and it goes on and on. Nobody seems to have any time to enjoy life.

And I am not saying that the new man will not work. He will work, but that will not be his addiction, he will not be a workaholic. It will not be a drug. He will work because he needs a few things, but he will not continuously work for more and more. He will not be accumulative. He will not believe in having a big bank balance, and he will not believe in being on a very high post. Rather, he would like to sing a song, play on the flute, on the guitar, dance. He would not like to become famous. He would like to live, authentically live. He will be ready to be a nobody.

And that is already happening. The first rays are already available. It is still hidden in the morning mist, but if you search you will find: the new children, the new generation, are a totally different kind of generation. Hence the generation gap, it is very real. It has never been so – never before has there been any generation gap. This is the first time in the whole of human history that there is a gap. The children are speaking a different language from their parents. The parents cannot understand because the parents want them to succeed. And the children say, "But what is the point of success if you cannot sing a song and you cannot dance, and you cannot enjoy and you cannot love, what is the point of being successful? Why? What is going to happen through success? Even if the whole world knows my name, what is that going to give me?"

The old generation believes in money. And you will be surprised that the belief in money is so deep that even those who renounce money also believe in money; otherwise there is no need to renounce it. And those who praise renunciation, they also believe in money: the more money you renounce, the greater you are. So the measurement is through money, money remains the criterion. In the world if you have more money you are great. And even in the world of the monks: "How much have you renounced?" If you have renounced more money, then you are more important. Money remains important even there.

The new generation is not going to be money-manic. And remember, I am not saying it is going to be against money – it will use money. In the past, money has used man; in the past, man has lived in such an unconscious way that he thought he possessed things, but things possessed him. The new man will be able to use: the new man will use money, will use technology, but the new man will remain the master. He is not going to become a victim, an instrument. This, according to me, is the greatest thing that is happening. A few characteristics...

The new consciousness is going to be counter to all orthodoxies – any kind of orthodoxy, Catholic or communist, Hindu or Jaina. Any kind of orthodoxy is a kind of paralysis of the mind – it paralyzes, you stop living. It becomes a rigidity around you. You become a fanatic, you become stubborn, you become rock-like. You don't behave like a liquid human being, you start behaving like a mule. You start behaving in a mule-ish way – stubborn, dead set, no possibility of changing, no flexibility, no fluidity. But in the past that has been praised very much: people call it consistency, certainty. It is not. It is neither consistency nor certainty. It is simply deadness.

An alive person has to remain flowing. He has to respond to the changing situations – and situations are continuously changing. How can you remain fixed in your attitudes when life itself is not fixed? When life is a river how can you remain stubborn? And if you remain stubborn you lose contact with life, you are already in your grave.

The new consciousness will be non-orthodox, non-fanatic. It will be fluid. It will not react, it will respond. And the difference between these two words is great.

Reaction is always rigid: you have a fixed idea, you react out of it; before the question is raised, the answer is ready. Response is totally different: you listen to the question, you absorb the question, you see the situation, you feel the situation, you live the situation and out of that very living, your response arises. A responsible man cannot be stubborn, cannot be certain, cannot be rigid. He will have to live moment to moment. He cannot decide beforehand. He will have to decide every day, each moment. And because he has to move continuously with life, its changing challenges, he cannot be consistent in the old sense. His consistency will be only one: that he will always be in tune with life. That will be his consistency, not that he has a certain idea and he remains consistent with that idea, and goes on sacrificing life for it.

There was a case against Mulla Nasrudin in the court and the magistrate asked him, "Mulla, how old are you?"

He said, "Forty."

The magistrate said, "But this is strange. You surprise me, because five years ago you were in court and that time also you said forty."

Mulla said, "Yes, I am a consistent man. Once I have said something, you can believe me. I will never say anything else."

This is one type of consistency. The new man will find it ridiculous. But the old man has been this way, consistent: in his character, in his statements, in his hypocrisy. The old man used to decide once and for all.

Psychologists say that almost fifty percent of your life is decided by the time you are seven years old – fifty percent! – and then you remain consistent with it. And life goes on changing – no wonder that you are left behind, that you start dragging, that you lose joy, that you lose the quality of dance. How can you dance? You are so far behind life, you are dead wood, you don't grow. An alive tree grows, changes; as the season changes, the tree changes. An alive person grows and continuously grows. To the very moment of death he goes on growing. He never knows any end to his growth.

Psychologists say the average mental age of man is thirteen. This is the situation, this is how the old man has lived up to now. A mental age of thirteen means at the age of thirteen people have stopped growing. Yes, they go on growing old, but they don't grow up. Growing old is one thing, growing up is totally different. Growing old is a physiological phenomenon, growing up means maturity, wisdom. And only those who go on flowing with life grow up.

The new man will not be obedient to stupid ideas that have been given from the past – and the ideas may not have been stupid when they were born, they may have been relevant in those circumstances. But as circumstances change, things become stupid. If you carry them, if you go on persisting in your old fixed routines, you start behaving in an absurd way.

Now, look: a religion is five thousand years old – that means five thousand years ago its rituals were born and since then they have remained fixed. How dangerous it is, how crippling! How can man be alive if these five-thousand-year-old rituals surround his soul?

The new man will be creative. Each moment he will find his religion, each moment he will find his philosophy, and everything will remain growing. He will not be obedient to the past, he cannot be. To be obedient to the past is to be obedient to death because the past is dead. He will be obedient to the present, and in being obedient to the present, he will be rebellious against the past.

To be rebellious is going to be one of his most prominent characteristics. And because he will be rebellious he will not fit in a dead society, he will not fit in a dead church, he will not fit in a dead army. He will not fit anywhere where obedience is a basic requirement. The new man is bound to create a new society around himself.

First consciousness becomes new, then the society becomes new. There is going to be a long period in which the old will resist the new, will fight with the new, will try to destroy the new. But the old cannot succeed. Time, time spirit, will not be in its favor – the old has to die. Just as the old body dies and makes space for a new child, so old societies, old orthodoxies, have to die. They have already lived overtime, they have lived too long.

The new consciousness will not be moralistic, will not be puritan – not that it will not have any morality. But it will have a different kind of morality – a morality that arises out of one's own feeling for life, one's sensitivity, one's own experiences; not a morality learned from others, borrowed. The new man will not be a man of character in the old sense because all character is binding. It creates an armor around you. The new man will be characterless in the sense that he will not have any armor. The new man will be characterless in the sense that he will not have a prison cell around him. Not that he will not have character, but he will give a new definition to character. He will not be a hypocrite.

The old puritanism, the old moralistic attitudes have created hypocrisy in the world. They have made man schizophrenic: on the surface one thing, deep within something else, almost the opposite. The old man lived a double life. The new man is going to live in a unitary way. He will live a single life. Whatever is inside him will also be his outside. He will be authentic. Remember this word *authenticity* – that is going to be the new man's religion. That is going to be the new man's truth, his temple, his God: authenticity. And with authenticity, neurosis disappears. The old man was neurotic because he was constantly in conflict: he wanted to do one thing and he was always doing something else, because something else was required. He was taught to do something against himself, he was repressive. His own authenticity was repressed and on top of it, a bogus character was imposed.

We have praised these phony people too long. Now the time has come: their phoniness should be exposed. We have praised these mahatmas and saints so long. Now we have to see their neurosis: they were all psychologically ill, they were pathological.

A healthy person is a whole person. His inside, his outside are the same. If he loves, he loves passionately; if he is angry, he is angry passionately. His anger has truth in it as much as his love has truth in it. The old man boils within and smiles on the outside. He lives without passion, without energy. He lives without any flame. His whole life is an exercise in phoniness and naturally he suffers. A long futile story is all that his life is: "...a tale told by an idiot, full of sound and fury, signifying nothing."

The new man will not be a tale told by an idiot but will be a poetry sung out of wholeness, will be a dance of immense joy for God's gift of life and being – for the flowers and the trees and the birds and the sun and the sand and the sea. The new man will not look somewhere far away for God. He will look here, close by. Now will be his only time, here will be his only space.

The new man will be earthly, and by "earthly" I don't mean materialistic. The new man will be a realist, he will love this earth. Because we have not loved this earth and our so-called religions have been teaching us to hate this earth, we have destroyed it. It is a beautiful planet, one of the most beautiful because it is one of the most alive. This planet has to be loved, this planet has to be rejoiced – it is a gift. This body has so many mysteries in it that even a Buddha is possible only because of this body. This body becomes the temple of the greatest possibility: buddhahood, nirvana. This body has to be loved, this earth has to be loved.

The new man will find his religion in nature – not in dead stone statues, but in living dancing trees in the wind. He will find his religion surfing the sea, climbing the virgin mountain. He will find his prayer with the snow, with the moon, with the stars. He will be in dialogue with existence as it is. He will not live with abstract ideas. He will live with realities. His commitment will be with nature, and through that commitment he will come to know super-nature. God is hidden here in this earth, in this very body: This very body the buddha, this very earth the paradise.

The new man will read the scripture of nature. This will be his Veda, his Koran, his Bible. Here he will find sermons in the stones. He will try to decipher the mysteries of life, he will not try to demystify life. He will try to love those mysteries, to enter those mysteries. He will be a poet, he will not be a philosopher. He will be an artist, he will not be a theologian. His science will also have a different tone. His science will be that of Tao – not an effort to conquer nature, because that effort is just foolish. How can you conquer nature? You are part of nature. His science will be of understanding nature, not of conquering nature. He will not rape nature, he will love and persuade nature to reveal its secrets.

The new man will not be ambitious, will not be political. Politics has no future. Politics has existed because of the neurosis of humankind. Once the neurosis disappears, politics will disappear.

Ambition simply means you are missing something and you are consoling yourself that in the future you will get it. Ambition is a consolation: today it is all misery, tomorrow there will be joy. Looking at tomorrow you become capable of tolerating today and its misery. Today is always hell, tomorrow is heaven: you keep on looking at heaven, you keep on hoping. But that hope is not going to be fulfilled ever because tomorrow never comes.

Ambition means you are incapable of transforming your today into a beatitude, you are impotent. Only impotent people are ambitious: they seek money, they seek power. Only impotent people seek power and money. The potential person lives. If money comes his way, he lives the money too, but he does not seek it, he is not after it. He is not afraid of it either.

The old man was either after money or afraid of money, either after power or afraid of power, but in both ways his whole focus was on power and money. He was ambitious. The old man is pitiable: he was ambitious because he was unable to live, unable to love. The new man will be able to live and able to love. And his herenow is going to be so beautiful, why should he be worried about tomorrow? His concern will not be having more, his concern will be being more – another very important distinction to be remembered. His concern will be being more, not having more. Having more is just a substitute for being more. You have more money – you think you are more. You have more power – you think you are more. Deep down you remain the same beggar. Alexander the Great dies as empty-handed as any beggar.

Being more is a totally different dimension. Being more means getting in touch with your reality, getting in tune with your being, and helping yourself to fall in harmony with the universe. To be in harmony with the universe you become more. The more you are in tune with existence, the more you are. If the harmony is total, you are a god. That's why we call Buddha a god, Mahavira a god: utter total harmony with existence, no conflict at all. They have dissolved themselves into the whole, they have become the whole, just as a dewdrop disappears into the ocean and becomes the ocean. They have died in their egos, now they live as existence itself.

The new man will have no use for sham, facade or pretense. He will be true because only through truth is liberation. All lies create bondages. Tell a single lie and you will have to tell a thousand and one to defend it, ad nauseam you will have to tell lies. Then there is no end to it: a single lie sooner or later will spread all over your being – it is like cancer.

Be truthful and you need not hide. You can be open. Be truthful – you need not protect yourself against existence. You can be vulnerable. In that vulnerability existence penetrates you, God reaches your heart.

Tell a lie and you are afraid. You will be afraid of God too, you will be afraid of facing him, you will be afraid of facing yourself. You will be continuously escaping – from yourself, from others, from God. You will be constantly hiding behind your pretensions, hypocrisy will become your lifestyle and that's where hell exists. Hypocrisy creates hell. Authenticity is the only joy – the only joy, I say. And if you are not authentic you will never be joyous.

The new consciousness will not put up with double-talk. The new consciousness will hate this kind of thing with a passion. This hatred for phoniness is the deepest mark of the new man. The new man will be opposed to structured, inflexible and infallible systems because life is a beautiful flow. It is not structured, it is freedom. It is not a prison, it is a temple. He would like organizations to be fluid, changing, adapting and human. Our states are inhuman, our armies are inhuman, our churches are inhuman. They dehumanize man, they reduce man into a thing because they don't respect man's freedom. The new man will respect his freedom and respect others' freedom too.

The old man is constantly interfering, poking his nose into everybody's affairs, trying to manipulate, criticizing, condemning, rewarding, punishing. The old man is continuously concerned with others: "What are you doing?" I was staying in Mumbai once. A Parsi woman came to me because just the day before I had criticized Satya Sai Baba and had called him a phony guru. She came to see me and she said, "I have come to tell you a few more things." She was thinking that I would be very happy because she had brought some information against Satya Sai Baba. She said, "He is a homosexual. And I know it from reliable sources."

I said, "But why should you be concerned? Homosexual or heterosexual – that is his business. It is his life. Who are you? Why should you be bothered about it?"

She was very shocked when I said that. She had come feeling that I would be very grateful to her because she was giving me such great information. Why should you be concerned? Can't you leave people to their own life? I criticize only when the other's life is concerned; otherwise there is no question. What Satya Sai Baba is doing with his sexuality is his business, it is nobody else's business. But the old man was constantly poking his nose into everybody's affairs.

Here it happens every day: the old kind of people come and they are very much in agony because some man is holding some woman's hand. Why? But he is not holding your hand. And if those two persons have decided to hold hands, they have absolute freedom to do that. And if they are enjoying, who are you to interfere? If the man is holding some woman's hand against her will, then maybe your help is needed, but if they both are willing then you should not be concerned at all.

But this is the old consciousness. It was always trying to find ways and means to manipulate others, to be dominant over others. The new consciousness will leave everyone to his own life. Unless somebody is harming others, he should not be prevented. Unless somebody is a danger to others, he should not be prevented. Unless somebody is interfering in somebody else's freedom, he should not be interfered with.

The old world remained without individuality – it hated individuality! It liked only sheep, crowds – people behaving in the same way and everybody following the same routine and the same structure. The new man will allow all kinds of possibilities. The new man will love liquid structures. He will be human, he will respect human beings. His respect will be almost religious.

The new man will have to find new forms of community, of closeness, of intimacy, of shared purpose, because the old society is not going to disappear immediately – it will linger. It will give all kinds of fight to the new society – as it always happens. It has so many vested interests, it cannot go easily. It will go only when it becomes impossible for it to remain in existence.

Before it goes, the new man will have to create new kinds of communes, new kinds of families, new communities of closeness, intimacy, shared purpose. That's why I am trying to create a small commune where you can be totally yourself – away from the structured and the rotten world – and you can be given absolute freedom. It will be an experimentation because on those lines, the future is going to move. It will be a small experiment but of immense significance.

The new consciousness will not have anything to do with institutions like marriage. The new man will have a natural distrust of marriage as an institution. A man–woman relationship has deep value for him only when it is a mutually enhancing, growing, flowing relationship. He will have little regard for marriage as a ceremony or for vows of permanence – which prove to be highly impermanent. He loves the moment and lives it in its totality. Marriage has no future. Love has a future.

In the past, love was not a reality, marriage was a reality. In the future, love is going to be the reality and marriage is going to become more and more unreal. In the past, people were married to each other, hence by and by they started liking and loving. In the future, people will love and like each other, only then will they live together. In the past to live together came first, and naturally when you live together a liking arises, a dependence arises. It was a need phenomenon; the husband needed the wife, the wife needed the husband, and then the children needed the parents to be together. It was more or less an economic phenomenon, but it was not out of love.

The future will know a different kind of relationship which is based purely on love and remains in existence only while love remains. And there is no hankering for its permanenc, because in life nothing is permanent; only plastic flowers are permanent. Real roses are born in the morning and are gone by the evening. And that is their beauty: they are beautiful when they come, they are beautiful when their petals start withering away. Their life is beautiful, their birth is beautiful, their death is beautiful, because there is aliveness. A plastic flower is never born, never lives, never dies.

Marriage has been a plastic flower in the past. The new consciousness can have no respect for marriage. It will have to create a new kind of intimacy – friendship – and it will have to learn to live with the impermanent phenomenon of love and of everything.

It needs guts to live with the impermanence of life because each time something changes you have to change yourself again. One wants to remain fixed – it seems safer, secure. That's how the old man has lived: the old man was not adventurous, his whole concern was security.

The new man will have the spirit of adventure. His concern will not be security, his concern will be ecstasy. He will not believe, because belief is a search for security – he will explore. He may not have neat answers to every question, but he will accept every challenge to inquiry, to exploration. He will go as far as life can take him. He will try to reach the stars. But he will remain open. He will not start with a belief, with a conclusion, he will start only with a quest, a question.

To start with a belief is not to start at all. To start with a belief is just playing a game with yourself. You have already believed – how can you explore? To explore one has to be agnostic, and that is going to be the religion of the future: agnosticism. One will be capable and courageous enough to say, "I don't know, but I am interested in knowing. And I am ready to go into any dimension, into any adventure."

The new man will be ready to risk. The old man was very businesslike, never ready to risk: risk was anathema, security was his goal. But with security you start dying. It is only in adventure, continuous adventure, that life grows to higher and higher plenitudes, that it reaches the Himalayan peaks.

The new person will be a spontaneous person – unpredictable, willing to risk newness, often willing to risk saying or doing the wild, the far-out thing. He will believe that everything is possible and anything can be tried. He will not cling to the known, he will always remain available to the unknown, even to the unknowable. And he will not sacrifice for any future because he will not be an idealist. He will not sacrifice for any abstract ideas, ideals, ideologies. He has a trust in his own experience and a profound distrust of all external authority.

The new man will trust only his own experience. Unless he knows, he will not trust it. No external authority can help the new man. Nobody can say, "I say so, so you have to believe. Because we have always believed, so you have to believe. Because our forefathers believed, so you have to believe. Because it is written in the Vedas and the Bible, you have to believe." The new man is not going to have anything to do with such nonsense. The new man will believe only if he knows. This is real trust: trust in one's own possibilities, potential. The new man will respect himself. To believe in external authorities is disrespectful toward one's own being.

And, finally, the new man will like to be close to elemental nature: to the sea, the sun, the snow, flowers, animals, birds, to life, growth, death.

This, according to me, is the most important phenomenon that is happening today: a new man is coming into existence, the first rays are already on the horizon. Prepare yourself to receive the new man, get ready – become a host to the guest who is going, just any moment, to knock on your doors. And that's what sannyas is all about: a preparation – getting ready to receive the new man. It is going to be a great adventure to receive the new man, it is going to be risky too because the old will not like it.

Now you can understand why the orthodox mind is against me: I am preparing their graveyard and I am preparing for something new – I am preparing a garden for the new. You are to open your hearts for the new, uproot all the weeds of the old, drop all the conditionings that the old has given to you so you can receive the new.

And remember, the days of the messiahs are over. Don't wait for Christ's coming again, and don't wait for Buddha's coming again. Nobody comes again, not at least Buddha and Christ. Those who come again are the people who live without learning anything from life. Buddha has learned the lesson – he will not be coming again. Christ has learned the lesson – he will not be coming again. Don't wait for any messiah to come, but wait for a new consciousness, not for a messiah to deliver you. That is what the old man used to believe: somebody will come. Hindus think Krishna will come: "When things are really dark and difficult and dismal, Krishna will come and deliver us." All nonsense! All holy cow dung!

A new consciousness is going to deliver you, not some person – Buddha, Krishna, Christ. They had been here and they could not deliver. No single person can do it – it is impossible. Only a new consciousness can deliver man from his bondage. And the new consciousness can come only through you: you have to become the womb, you have to accept it, receive it, prepare yourself for it.

Sannyas is nothing but getting ready for something immensely valuable, so that when the gift comes you are not fast asleep, so when the new consciousness knocks on your door you are ready to embrace it.

I am neither Sufi nor Zen. I am neither male nor female. I am neither positive nor negative. And I am here to help you to transcend all polarities. Hence I speak on the polarities, so that you can understand them, so that you can become aware of them – so much so that you are not trapped by them.

I talk to you about Sufism and about Zen so that one day you can go beyond both. You have to go beyond all standpoints! You have to go beyond all kinds of principles, dogmas, paths, methods, techniques. To be with me is on the way toward transcendence. I am neither a theist nor an atheist, neither a Hindu nor a Mohammedan.

I am simply an awareness – full of love. You can also become that because whatever I have become, you can become, because wherever you are, I was also there one day, with the same agony, the same suffering, with the same dichotomies – with the same problems! I was just like you. That's why I say you can also be just like me.

Beyond the Binary

> Some days I feel like a man and others like a woman. Can I be both? Or will I grow up schizy?

Everybody is both, and you have become aware of it. That's very good, that's a great insight into your being. Everybody is both but up to now the society has been conditioned in such a way, we have been taught and brought up in such a way that man is man, woman is woman. This is a very false arrangement, untrue to nature. If a man starts crying and weeping, people start telling him, "Don't weep like a woman, don't cry like a woman; don't be sissy." This is nonsense – because a man has as many tear glands in his eye as a woman. If nature had not meant him to cry and weep then there would have been no tear glands.

Now this is very repressive. If a girl starts behaving like a man, is ambitious, aggressive, people start thinking that something is wrong: something hormonal is wrong. They call her a tomboy; she is not a girl. This is nonsense! This division is not natural; this division is political, social.

Women have been forced to play the role of women twenty-four hours a day, and men have been forced to play the role of men twenty-four hours a day – which is very unnatural and certainly creates much misery in the world.

There are moments when a man is soft and should be feminine. There are moments when the husband should be the wife and the wife should be the husband, and this should be very natural. And there will be more rhythm and more harmony. If a man is not *supposed* to be a man twenty-four hours a day, he will be more relaxed.

And if a woman is not supposed to be a woman twenty-four hours a day, she will be more natural and spontaneous.

Yes, sometimes in a rage a woman becomes more dangerous than a man, and sometimes in soft moments a man is more loving than any woman – and these moments go on changing. Both these climates are yours; so don't think that you are becoming schizophrenic or something. This duality is part of nature.

A good insight has happened to you. Don't lose it and don't be worried that you are going schizophrenic. It is a shift: a few hours you are man, a few hours you are woman. If you watch it exactly you can know exactly how many minutes you are a man and how many minutes you are a woman. It is a periodical change. In yoga they have worked hard on these inner secrets. If you watch your breath, that will give you the exact time. When one nostril, the left nostril, is breathing you are feminine. When the right nostril is breathing you are male. And after nearabout forty-eight minutes they change.

Continuously – day and night – this change happens. When you are breathing by the left nostril your right-brain hemisphere functions: the right is the feminine part. When you are breathing from the right nostril your left brain functions: that is the male part. And sometimes you can play games with it.

If you are very angry then do one thing: close your right nostril and start breathing by the left, and within seconds you will see the anger has disappeared – because to be angry you need to be in the male part of your being. Try it and you will be surprised. Just by changing the breath from one nostril to another something of tremendous importance changes. If you are feeling very cold toward the world then breathe from the left nostril and let your imagination, fantasy, warmth flow in – and you will suddenly feel full of warmth.

And there are acts which can be done more easily when you are in the male climate. When you are doing something hard – carrying a rock, pushing a rock – check your nostril. If it is not in the male climate it is not good. It may be dangerous for the body: you will be very soft. When you are playing with a child, or just sitting with your dog, feel that you are in the feminine – more affinity will arise. When you are writing a poem or painting or making music you should be in the feminine – unless you are trying to create war music! Then it is okay, you should be in the male climate – aggressive.

Watch it, and you will be becoming more and more aware of

these two polarities. And this is good that these two polarities exist: that's how nature arranges for rest. When the male part becomes tired you move to the female part; the male part rests. When the female part is tired you rest; you become male. And this is an inner economy – one goes on changing. But your society has taught you wrong things: that a man is a man, and *has* to be a man twenty-four hours a day – this is too much of a duty. And a woman has to be a woman twenty-four hours a day – soft, loving, compassionate: this is too much of a duty. Sometimes she also wants to fight, be angry, throw things. And this is good, if you understand the inner play.

These two polarities are a good inner play – the play of consciousness. This is how God has become divided in you, to have a play of hide-and-seek with himself. When the play is over, when you have learned that which is to be learned from the play, when the lesson has been learned, then you pass beyond.

The ultimate stage is neither male nor female: it is neutral.

Masculinity can have two directions, just as femininity can have two directions. The masculine mind can be aggressive, violent, destructive – that is only one of the possibilities. Men have tried that, and humanity has suffered much from it.
But there is a positive aspect. Nothing can be only negative; every negativity has a positive aspect too. Every dark cloud has a silver lining, and every night is followed by the morning.
Positive masculinity is initiative, creativity, adventure. These are the same qualities, but moving on a different plane. The negative masculine mind becomes destructive, the positive masculine mind becomes creative. Destructiveness and creativeness are not two things, but two aspects of one energy. The same energy can become aggression and the same energy can become initiative.
When aggression is initiative it has a beauty of its own. When violence becomes adventure, when violence becomes exploration, exploration of the new, of the unknown, it is tremendously beneficial.

The Creator

In the past all famous artists have been well-known for their bohemian style of life. Please can you say something about creativity and discipline?

The bohemian life is the only life worth living! All other kinds of lives are only lukewarm; they are more ways of committing slow suicide than ways of living life passionately and intensely. In the past it was inevitable that the artist had to live in rebellion, because creativity is the greatest rebellion in existence. If you want to create you have to get rid of all conditionings; otherwise your creativity will be nothing but copying, it will be just a carbon copy. You can be creative only if you are an individual, you cannot create as a part of the mob psychology. The mob psychology is uncreative; it lives a life that is more of a drag. It knows no dance, no song, no joy; it is mechanical.

Of course, there are a few things you will get from the society only if you are mechanical. Respectability you will get, honors you will get. Universities will confer DLitts on you, countries will give you gold medals, you may finally become a Nobel laureate. But this whole thing is ugly.

A real man of genius will discard all this nonsense because this is bribery. Giving the Nobel Prize to a person simply means: your services to the establishment are respected, you are honored because you have been a good slave, obedient, you have not gone astray, you have followed the well-trodden path.

The creator cannot follow the well-trodden path. He has to search and find his own way. He has to inquire in the jungles of life, he has to go alone, he has to be a dropout from the mob mind, from the collective psychology. The collective mind is the lowest mind in the world; even the so-called idiots are a little more superior than the collective idiocy. But the collectivity has its own bribes: it respects people, honors people, if they go on insisting that the way of the collective mind is the only right way.

It was out of sheer necessity that in the past, creators of all kinds – the painters, the dancers, the musicians, the poets, the sculptors – had to renounce respectability. They had to live a kind of bohemian life, the life of a vagabond; that was the only possibility for them to be creative. This need not be so in the future. If you understand me, if you feel what I am saying has truth in it, then in the future everybody should live individually and there will be no need for a bohemian life. The bohemian life is the by-product of a fixed, orthodox, conventional, respectable life.

My effort is to destroy the collective mind and to make each individual free to be himself or herself. Then there is no problem; then you can live as you want to live. In fact, humanity will really only be born the day the individual is respected in his rebellion. Humanity has still not been born; it is still in the womb. What you see as humanity is only a very hocus-pocus phenomenon. Unless we give individual freedom to each person, absolute freedom to each person to be himself, to exist in his own way... And, of course, he has not to interfere with anybody – that is part of freedom. Nobody should interfere with anybody.

But in the past everybody has been poking his nose into everybody else's affairs – even into things which are absolutely private, which have nothing to do with the society. For example, you fall in love with a woman – what has that got to do with the society? It is purely a personal phenomenon, it is not of the marketplace. If two people are agreeing to commune in love, the society should not come into it. But the society comes into it with all its paraphernalia, in direct ways, in indirect ways. The policeman will stand between the lovers; the magistrate will stand between the lovers; and if that is not enough then the societies have created a super-policeman, God, who will take care of you.

The idea of God is that of a peeping Tom who does not even allow you privacy in your bathroom, who goes on looking through the keyhole, watching what you are doing. This is ugly. All the religions of the world say God continuously watches you – this is ugly. What kind of God is this? Has he got no other business but to watch everybody, follow everybody? Seems to be the supreme-most detective!

Humanity needs a new soil – the soil of freedom. Bohemianism was a reaction, a necessary reaction, but if my vision succeeds then there will be no bohemianism because there will be no so-called collective mind trying to dominate people. Then everybody will be at ease with himself. Of course, you have not to interfere with anybody, but as far as your life is concerned you have to live it on your own terms. Only then is there creativity. Creativity is the fragrance of individual freedom.

You ask me: "Please can you say something about creativity and discipline?" *Discipline* is a beautiful word, but it has been misused as all other beautiful words have been misused in the past. The word *discipline* comes from the same root as the word *disciple*; the root meaning of the word is "a process of learning." One who is ready to learn is a disciple, and the process of being ready to learn is discipline.

The knowledgeable person is never ready to learn because he already thinks he knows; he is very centered in his so-called knowledge. His knowledge is nothing but a nourishment for his ego. He cannot be a disciple, he cannot be in true discipline.

Socrates says: "I know only one thing, that I know nothing." That is the beginning of discipline. When you don't know anything, of course, a great longing to inquire, explore, investigate arises. And the moment you start learning, another factor follows inevitably: whatever you have learned has to be dropped continuously, otherwise it will become knowledge and knowledge will prevent further learning.

The real man of discipline never accumulates; each moment he dies to whatever he has come to know and again becomes ignorant. That ignorance is really luminous. It is one of the most beautiful experiences in existence to be in a state of luminous not-knowing. When you are in that state of not-knowing you are open. There is no barrier, you are ready to explore. The Hindus cannot do it; they are already knowledgeable. The Mohammedans cannot do it, the Christians cannot do it.

Discipline has been misinterpreted. People have been telling others to discipline their life, to do this, not to do that. Thousands of shoulds and should-nots have been imposed on man, and when a man lives with thousands of shoulds and should-nots he cannot be creative. He is a prisoner; everywhere he will come across a wall.

The creative person has to dissolve all shoulds and should-nots. He needs freedom and space, vast space, he needs the whole sky and all the stars, only then can his innermost spontaneity start growing.

So remember, my meaning of discipline is not that of any Ten Commandments. I am not giving you any discipline; I am simply giving you an insight into how to remain learning and never become knowledgeable. Your discipline has to come from your very heart, it has to be *yours* – and there is a great difference. When somebody else gives you the discipline it can never fit you; it will be like wearing somebody else's clothes. Either they will be too loose or too tight, and you will always feel a little bit silly in them.

Mohammed has given a discipline to the Mohammedans; it may have been good for him, but it cannot be good for anybody else. Buddha has given a discipline to millions of Buddhists; it may have been good for him, but it cannot be good for anybody else. A discipline is an individual phenomenon; whenever you borrow it you start living according to set principles, dead principles. And life is never dead; life is constantly changing each moment. Life is a flux.

Heraclitus is right: you cannot step in the same river twice. In fact, I myself would like to say you cannot step in the same river even once, the river is so fast moving! One has to be alert to, watchful of, each situation and its nuances, and one has to respond to the situation according to the moment, not according to any readymade answers given by others.

Do you see the stupidity of humanity? Five thousand years ago Manu gave a discipline to the Hindus and they are still following it. Three thousand years ago Moses gave a discipline to the Jews and they are still following it. Five thousand years ago Adinatha gave his discipline to the Jainas and they are still following it. The whole world is being driven crazy by these disciplines! They are out of date, they should have been buried long long ago. You are carrying corpses and those corpses are stinking. And when you live surrounded by corpses, what kind of life can you have?

I teach you the moment, and the freedom of the moment, and the responsibility of the moment. One thing may be right this moment and may become wrong the next moment. Don't try to be consistent, otherwise you will be dead. Only dead people are consistent.

Try to be alive, with all its inconsistencies, and live each moment without any reference to the past, without any reference to the future either. Live the moment in the context of the moment, and your response will be total. And that totality has beauty and that totality is creativity. Then whatever you do will have a beauty of its own.

The Watcher

There was a man of Wei, Tung-Men Wu, who did not grieve when his son died.
His wife said to him: "No one in the world loved his son as much as you did, why do you not grieve now he is dead?"
He answered: "I had no son, and when I had no son I did not grieve. Now that he is dead it is the same as it was before, when I had no son. Why should I grieve over him?"

The most fundamental religious truth is that man is asleep – not physically, but metaphysically; not apparently, but deep down. Man lives in a deep slumber. He works, he moves, he thinks, he imagines, he dreams, but the sleep continues as a basic substratum of his life. Rare are the moments when you feel really awake – very rare; they can be counted on the fingers. If in seventy years' life you have only seven moments of awakening, that too will be too much.

Man lives like a robot: mechanically efficient, but with no awareness; hence the whole problem. There are so many problems man has to face, but they are all by-products of his sleep.

So the first thing to be understood is what this sleep consists in – because Zen is an effort to become alert and awake. All religion is nothing but that: an effort to become more conscious, an effort to become more aware, an effort to bring more alertness, attentiveness to your life.

All the religions of the world, in one way or another, emphasize that the sleep consists in deep identification or in attachment.

Man's life has two layers to it: one is that of the essential, and another is that of the accidental. The essential is never born, never dies. The accidental is born, lives, and dies. The essential is eternal, timeless; the accidental is just accidental. We become too much attached to the accidental and we tend to forget the essential.

A man becomes too much attached to money – money is accidental. It has nothing to do with essential life. A man becomes too much attached to his house or to his car, or to his wife, or to her husband, to children, to relationship. Relationship is accidental; it has nothing essential in it. It is not your real being. And in this century, the twentieth century, the problem has become too deep.

There are people who call the twentieth century "the accidental century" – they are right. People are living too much identified with the nonessential: money, power, prestige, respectability. You will have to leave all that behind when you go. Even an Alexander has to go empty-handed.

I have heard...

A great mystic died. When he reached paradise, he asked God why Jesus was not born in the twentieth century.

The Lord God started laughing and said, "Impossible! Impossible! Where would the twentieth-century people ever find three wise men or a virgin?"

The twentieth century is the most accidental. By and by, man has become too much attached to "my" and "mine" – to possessions. And he has completely lost track of his being. He has completely lost track of "I." "My" has become more important. When "my" becomes more important, you are getting attached to the accidental. When "I" remains more important and "my" remains just as a servant, then you are a master, then you are not a slave – then you live in a totally different way.

That's what Zen people call the original face of man, where pure "I" exists. This "I" has nothing to do with the ego. Ego is nothing but the center of all the nonessential possessions that you have. The ego is nothing but the accumulated "my" and "mine" – my house, my car, my prestige, my religion, my scripture, my character, my morality, my family, my heritage, my tradition. All these "my's," all these "mines" go on accumulating; they become crystallized as the ego.

When I am using the word "I," I am using it in an absolutely non-egoistic sense. "I" means your being.

Zen people say: Find out your face, the face you had before you were born; find out that face that you will again have when you are dead. Between birth and death, whatever you think is your face is accidental. You have seen it in a mirror; you have not felt it from the within – you have looked for it in the without. Do you know your original face? You know only the face your mirror shows to you. And all our relationships are just mirrors.

The husband says to the wife, "You are beautiful" and she starts thinking she is beautiful. Somebody comes, buttresses you, says, "You are very wise, intelligent, a genius!" and you start believing in it. Or somebody condemns you, hates you, is angry about you. You don't accept what he says, but still, deep down in the unconscious it goes on accumulating. Hence the ambiguity of man.

Somebody says you are beautiful, somebody else says you are ugly – now what to do? One mirror says you are wise, another man says you are an idiot – now what to do? You depend only on mirrors, and both are mirrors. You may not like the mirror that says you are an idiot, but it has said so, it has done its work. You may repress it, you may never bring it to your consciousness, but deep down it will remain in you that a mirror has said you are an idiot.

You trust in mirrors – then you become split because there are so many mirrors. And each mirror has its own investment. Somebody calls you wise – not because you are wise; he has his own investment. Somebody calls you an idiot – not because you are an idiot; he has his own investment. They are simply showing their likes and dislikes; they are not asserting anything about you. They may be asserting something about themselves, maybe, but they are not saying anything about you – because no mirror can show you who you are.

Mirrors can only show you your surface, your skin. You are not on your skin; you are very deep. You are not your body. One day the body is young, another day it becomes old. One day it is beautiful, healthy; another day it becomes crippled and paralyzed. One day you were throbbing with life; another day life has oozed out of you. But you are not your periphery – you are your center.

The accidental man lives on the periphery. The essential man remains centered. This is the whole effort.

Let me tell you an anecdote; I have heard a very beautiful Jewish story – it is tremendously significant.

It is about a man who was always sleepy, and always ready to sleep – everywhere. At the biggest mass meetings, at all the concerts, at every important convention, he could be seen sitting asleep.

You must have known that man because you are that. And you must have come across that man many, many times, because how can you avoid him? It is you.

...And he slept in every conceivable and inconceivable pose. He slept with his elbows in the air and his hands behind his head. He slept standing up, leaning against himself so that he should not fall down. He slept in the theater, in the streets, in the synagogue. Wherever he went, his eyes would drip with sleep.

Had he been a Hindu he could have even slept standing on his head in *shirshasana*. I have seen Hindus sleeping that way. Many yogis become efficient in sleeping standing on their head. It is difficult, arduous, it needs great practice – but it happens.

...Neighbors used to say that he had already slept through several big fires. And once, during a really big fire, he was carried out of his bed, still asleep, and put down on the sidewalk. In this way he slept for several hours until a patrol came along and took him away.

It was said that when he was standing under the wedding canopy and reciting the vows – "Thou art to me..." – he fell asleep at the word *sanctified* – try to remember him! – and they had to beat him over the head with brass pestles for several hours to wake him up. And he slowly said the next word and again fell asleep.

Remember your own wedding ceremony. Remember your honeymoon. Remember your marriage. Have you ever been awake? Have you ever missed any opportunity where you could have fallen asleep? You have always fallen asleep. We mention all this so that you may believe the following story about our hero.

...Once, when he went to sleep, he slept and slept and slept. But in his sleep it seemed to him that he heard thunder in the streets and his bed was shaking somewhat. So he thought in his sleep that it was raining outside, and as a result his sleep became still more delicious. He wrapped himself up in his quilt and in its warmth.

Do you remember how many times you have interpreted things through your sleep? Do you remember sometimes you have fixed the alarm clock, and when it goes off you start dreaming that you are in the church and the bells are ringing? A trick of the mind to avoid the alarm, to avoid the disturbance that the alarm is creating.

When he awoke he saw a strange void: his wife was no longer there, his bed was no longer there, his quilt was no longer there. He wanted to look through the window, but there was no window to look through. He wanted to run down the three flights and yell "Help!" – but there were no stairs to run on and no air to yell in. And when he wanted merely to go out of doors, he saw that there was no out of doors – everything had evaporated!

For a while he stood there in confusion unable to comprehend what had happened. But afterward he thought to himself: I will go to sleep. He saw, however, that there was no longer any earth to sleep on. Only then did he raise two fingers to his forehead and reflect: Apparently I have slept through the end of the world – isn't that a fine how-do-you-do?

He became depressed. No more world, he thought. What will I do without a world? Where will I go to work, how will I make a living, especially now that the cost of living is so high and a dozen eggs costs a dollar twenty – and who knows if they are even fresh? And besides, what will happen to the five dollars the gas company owes me? And where has my wife gone off to? Is it possible that she too has disappeared with the world, and with the thirty dollars' pay I had in my pockets? And she is not by nature the kind that disappears, he thought to himself.

You will also think that way one day if you suddenly find the world has disappeared. You don't know what else to think. You will think about the cost of eggs, the office, the wife, money. You don't know what else to think about. The whole world has disappeared – but you have become mechanical in your thinking.

...And what will I do if I want to sleep? What will I stretch out on if there isn't any world? And maybe my back will ache? And who will finish the bundle of work in the shop? And suppose I want a glass of malted – where will I get it?

Ah, he thought, have you ever seen anything like it? A man should fall asleep with the world under his head and wake up without it?

This is going to happen one day or another; that's what happens to every man when he dies. Suddenly, the whole world disappears. Suddenly he is no longer part of this world; suddenly he is in another dimension. This happens to every man who dies – because whatever you have known is just the peripheral. When you die, suddenly your periphery disappears – you are thrown to your center. And you don't know that language. And you don't know anything about the center. It looks like void, empty. It feels like just a negation, an absence.

...As our hero stood there in his underwear, wondering what to do, a thought occurred to him: To hell with it! So there isn't any world – who needs it anyway? Disappeared is disappeared; I might as well go to the movies and kill some time. But to his astonishment he saw that, together with the world, the movies had also disappeared.

A pretty mess I've made here, thought our hero, and began smoothing his mustache. A pretty mess I've made here, falling asleep. If I hadn't slept so soundly, he taunted himself, I would have disappeared along with everything else. This way I'm unfortunate, and where will I get a malted? I love a glass in the morning. And my wife? Who knows who she has disappeared with? If it is with the presser from the top floor, I'll murder her, so help me God.

Who knows how late it is? With these words our hero wanted to look at his watch but couldn't find it. He searched with both hands in the left and right pockets of the infinite emptiness but could find nothing to touch.

I just paid two dollars for a watch, and here it has already disappeared. He thought to himself: All right. If the world went under, it went under. That I don't care about. It isn't my world. But the watch? Why should my watch go under? A new watch – two dollars – it wasn't even wound.

And where will I find a glass of malted? There's nothing better in the morning than a glass of malted. And who knows if my wife... I've slept through such a terrible catastrophe, I deserve the worst. Help... Help ...Help! Where are my brains? Where were my brains before? Why didn't I keep an eye on the world and my wife? Why did I let them disappear when they were still so young?

And our hero began to beat his head against the void – but since the void was a very soft one it didn't hurt him and he remained alive to tell the story.

This is a story of human mind as such. You create a world around you of illusions. You go on getting attached to things which are not going to be with you when you die. You go on being identified with things which are going to be taken away from you.

Hence, the Hindus call the world "illusion." They don't mean by "the world" the world that is there – they simply mean the world that you have created out of your sleep. That world is maya – illusion. It is a dream world.

Who is your wife? The very idea is foolish. Who is your husband? Who is your child? You are not yours – how can anybody else be yours? Not even you are yours; not even you belong to yourself. Have you watched sometimes that not even you belong to yourself? You also belong to some unknown existence you have not penetrated.

Deeper in yourself you will come to a point where even self disappears: only a state of no-self, or call it the "supreme self" – it is only a difference of language and terminology. Have you not seen, deep down in yourself, things arising which don't belong to you? Your desires don't belong to you, your thoughts don't belong to you. Even your consciousness, you have not created it – it has been given to you, it is a given fact. It is not you who has created it – how can you create it?

You are suddenly there, as if it happens by magic. You are always in the middle; you don't know the beginning. The beginning does not belong to you, and neither does the end belong to you. Just in the middle you can create, you can go on creating dreams. That's how a man becomes accidental.

Watch. Become more and more essential and less and less accidental. Always remember: only that which is eternal is true; only that which is going to be forever and ever is true. That which is momentary is untrue. The momentary has to be watched and not to be identified with.

I was reading a beautiful anecdote...

An elderly Irishman checked out of a hotel room and was halfway to the bus depot when he realized he had left his umbrella behind. By the time he got back to the room, a newly-wed couple had already checked in. Hating to interrupt anything, the Irishman got down on his knees and listened in at the keyhole.

"Whose lovely eyes are those, my darling?" he heard the man's voice ask.

"Yours, my love," the woman answered.

"And whose precious nose is this?" the man went on inside the room.

"Only yours," the woman replied.

"And whose beautiful lips are these?" the man continued.

"Yours!" panted the woman.

"And whose...?" but the Irishman could not stand it anymore.

Putting his mouth to the keyhole, he shouted, "When you come to a yellow plaid umbrella, folks, it's mine!"

This game of "my" and "mine" is the most absurd game – but this is the whole game of life. This earth was there before you ever came here, and it will be here when you are gone. The diamonds that you possess were there before you ever came here, and when you are gone those diamonds will remain here – and they will not even remember you. They are completely oblivious that you possess them.

This game of possessiveness is the most foolish game there is – but this is the whole game.

Gurdjieff used to say that if you start getting disidentified from things, sooner or later you will fall upon your essential being. That is the basic meaning of renunciation. Renunciation does not mean, sannyas does not mean, renouncing the world and escaping to the Himalayas or to a monastery – because if you escape from the world and go to a monastery, nothing is going to change. You carry the same mind. Here in the world, the house was yours and the wife was yours; there, the monastery will be yours, the religion will be yours. It will not make much difference. The "mine" will persist. It is a mind attitude – it has nothing to do with any outside space. It is an inner illusion, an inner dream, an inner sleep.

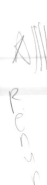

Renunciation means: wherever you are, there is no need to renounce the things because in the first place you never possessed them. It is foolish to talk about renunciation – as if you were the possessor and now you are renouncing. How can you renounce something which you never possessed? Renunciation means coming to know that you cannot possess anything. You can use, at the most, but you cannot possess. You are not going to be here forever – how can you possess? It is impossible to possess anything. You can use and you can be grateful to things that they allow themselves to be used. You should be thankful to things that they allow themselves to be used. They become means, but you cannot possess them.

Dropping the idea of ownership is renunciation. Renunciation is not dropping the possessions but possessiveness. And this is what Gurdjieff calls getting unidentified. This is what Bauls call realizing *adhar manush* – the essential man. This is what Zen people call the original face.

There is a very famous Taoist story – I love it tremendously...

The story is about an old Taoist farmer whose horse ran away. That evening the neighbors gathered to commiserate with him since this was such bad luck. He said, "Maybe...."

The next day the horse returned, but brought with it six wild horses, and the neighbors came exclaiming at the good fortune. He said, "Maybe...."

And then the following day, his son tried to saddle and ride one of the wild horses, was thrown, and broke his leg. Again the neighbors came to offer their sympathy for the misfortune. He said, "Maybe...."

The day after that, conscription officers came to the village to seize young men for the army, but because of the broken leg the farmer's son was rejected. When the neighbors came in to say how fortunate everything had turned out, he said, "Maybe...."

This is the attitude of a man who understands what is accidental and what is essential. The accidental is always "maybe"; it is a "perhaps." You cannot be certain about it, you need not be certain about it. People who become certain about the accidental are going to be frustrated sooner or later; their certainty is going to create much frustration for them. Their certainty will create expectations, and they cannot be fulfilled because the universe is not there to fulfill your expectations. It has its own destiny. It is moving toward its own goal. It does not care about your private goals.

All private goals are against the goal of the universe itself. All private goals are against the goal of the whole. All private goals are neurotic. The essential man comes to know, to feel, "I am not separate from the whole, and there is no need to seek and search for any destiny on my own. Things are happening, the world is moving – call it the universal reality – it is doing things. They are happening of their own accord. There is no need for me to make any struggle, any effort; there is no need for me to fight for anything. I can relax and be."

The essential man is not a doer. The accidental man is a doer. The accidental man is, of course, then in anxiety, tension, stress, anguish, continuously sitting on a volcano – it can erupt any moment because he lives in a world of uncertainty, yet believes as if it is certain. This creates tension in his being; he knows deep down that nothing is certain. A rich man has everything that he can have, and yet he knows deep down that he has nothing. That's what makes a rich man even poorer than a poor man.

A poor man is never so poor because still he has hopes – some day or other, destiny is going to shower blessings on him; some day or other he will be able to arrive, to achieve. He can hope. The rich man has arrived, his hopes are fulfilled – now, suddenly, he finds nothing is fulfilled. All hopes fulfilled and yet nothing is fulfilled. He has arrived and he has not arrived at all – it has always been a dream journey. He has not moved a single inch.

A man who is successful in the world feels the pain of being a failure as nobody else can feel it. There is a proverb that says that nothing succeeds like success. I would like to tell you: Nothing fails like success. But you cannot know it unless you have succeeded. When all the riches are there that you dreamed about, planned about, worked hard for, then sitting just amidst those riches is the beggar – deep inside empty, hollow; nothing inside, everything outside.

In fact, when everything is there outside, it becomes a contrast. It simply emphasizes your inner emptiness and nothingness. It simply emphasizes your inner beggarliness, poverty. A rich man knows poverty as no poor man can ever know. A successful man knows what failure is. At the top of the world, suddenly you realize that you have been behaving foolishly. You may not say so, because what is the point of saying it? You may go on pretending that you are very happy – presidents and prime ministers go on pretending they are very happy; they are not. They are just saving their faces. Now, what to say? There is no point even in saying anything – they are not true.

In the older ages, people were truer, more authentic. Buddha was a prince, he was going to be the emperor, but he realized that there is nothing in it. He could have pretended. Mahavira was a prince, he was going to be the emperor. He realized that there is nothing in it. They simply declared their realization to the world. They simply said that riches have failed, that kingdoms are not kingdoms; that if you are really seeking the kingdom, you will have to seek somewhere else, in some other direction.

In this world there is no way to arrive.

It happened...

Theodore Roosevelt, returning from Africa, received a most affectionate and exuberant greeting as his ship steamed into New York harbor. Bands were playing; soldiers, sailors, and marines saluted; pretty girls greeted him as pretty girls will do. Ships in the harbor sprayed water in a festive white arc, and the people – throngs of people – shouted their welcome to him.

On the same ship, a mystic, a very old wise man, was also returning. A few old friends greeted him off in a corner, trying to be heard in the tumultuous noise. One of them said, "We are sorry we can't welcome you home as Theodore Roosevelt is being welcomed."

To which the mystic answered as he pointed upward, "That's all right – I'm not home yet."

In this world there is no home. This world is accidental. It is illusory – just ripples on the surface, waves. And whatever you are doing is nothing but making card houses, or trying to sail paper boats: they are doomed to drown. This realization makes a man a little alert for the first time about his sleepiness, and then he starts moving more and more toward consciousness.

When things are no longer important, only consciousness becomes important. When things are no longer significant, a new search, a new door opens. Then you are not rushing toward the without; you start slipping into the within. The kingdom of god is within. And once you drop identifying with things, suddenly you are no longer fighting – there is no point. You start moving with the river of existence.

Arrival at home is effortless.

Bodhi has sent me a small, beautiful story; Werner Erhard likes to tell it:

Once there was a famous medicine man in Northern Canada who was said to have enormous powers. When he waved a blanket at the Northern Lights they changed color. Every time he waved his blanket, the Northern Lights really would change color.

One day, he lost his blanket and the Northern Lights changed color anyway. That ruined his reputation as a medicine man.

Life is also that way. No matter what you do, life only turns out the way it turns out. Struggling with life does not help at all.

Struggling is simply destructive; there is no point in it. Effort is not needed. Effort is needed only in the accidental world and even there too it fails finally; eventually it fails. It gives you hope, but eventually it fails.

In the inner world no effort is needed. Once you start slipping withinward, you suddenly see everything is happening as it should. Life is perfect. There is no way to improve upon it. Then celebration starts.

When life is felt as perfect, when you suddenly see the tremendous beatitude, the tremendous glory surrounding you; when you suddenly see that you have always been at home – there was nowhere else to go... When you suddenly feel in your innermost core of being that you are with the divine and the divine is with you, that you are floating with the whole, you don't have a private destiny – the destiny of the whole is your destiny also, so wherever this existence is moving, you are also moving; you don't have any private goals – you are no longer idiotic.

The word *idiot* is very beautiful. It comes from the same root as *idiom*. It means a person who is trying to live a private life, a person who is trying to move against the whole. A person who has his own idiom – that's what an idiot is. The whole world is going to the south, he is going to the north – that's what an idiot is.

The accidental man is idiotic. Such a vast universe, running so smoothly...look at the stars, look at the change of seasons; rivers running from the Himalayas to the ocean, clouds coming and showering. Watch nature: everything is running so smoothly. Why not become a part of it? Why create any conflict? Conflict creates anxiety; anxiety brings anguish.

If you have a private goal you are going to go mad. Relax! Drop out of the accidental world so you can drop into the essential world. Then one starts accepting things as they are. Then one starts loving things as they are. Then one starts cherishing things as they are. And they have always been beautiful.

Once you are not fighting, not going anywhere, you can feel the music, the surrounding celestial music. You can see the infinite beauty and you can feel grateful for it. It is a gift. There is no need to steal it – it is already given to you. By being alive, existence has already accepted you. By being alive, the divine has already loved you.

If you don't like the word *divine*, you can drop it. I am not a fanatic about language. You can call it "existence," "the unknown," "the truth," "the ultimate," "the absolute" – or anything. Any name will do – *X*, *Y*, *Z* – because it has no name. It is not particular so it cannot have any name; it is not particular so it cannot have any adjective. It is the universal. It is that which is.

So there are two ways of living. One is the accidental way. The accidental way is the worldly way. The worldly way is against existence, against the whole. Then there is another way of living, another style – tremendously graceful, with no anxiety, no anguish.

I have heard...

A botanist, a great scientist, came across a valley in the Himalayas where beautiful flowers were flowering, but there was no path. It was very difficult to reach into the valley, thousands of feet down. And he had never heard about these flowers. He had studied about all flowers; this was some new species, undiscovered. He was enchanted, intrigued. He wanted to get those flowers but there was no way – what to do?

In a desperate effort, he took his small child, tied a rope under the child's arms and dropped him into the valley. The botanist was afraid, perspiring, trembling...something may go amiss.

And then the child reached the valley and picked a few flowers. The father shouted from the top of the hill: "Are you okay, my son? Are you not afraid?"

The son laughed. He said, "Why should I be afraid? The rope is in my father's hands."

The father may be afraid, but the child is not afraid. That's what a religious man feels: The rope is in my father's hands. Then suddenly all anxiety disappears.

In the accidental world you have to struggle. In the essential world you have simply to surrender. In the accidental world you have to doubt. In the essential world you simply trust – and this trust is not like belief. Belief is against doubt. Trust is simply the absence of doubt – it is not against doubt. You simply feel trustful.

So the question is not how to believe. The question is how to change your consciousness from being accidental to essential, how to come to your center, how to start feeling your center again. Trust will arise – trust is an outcome, a by-product. When one comes closer to one's center, one starts trusting more and more.

But ordinarily our whole training is how to fight. We have been trained as soldiers. As I see it there are only two types of people in the world – the soldiers and the sannyasins. The soldiers are those who have been taught to fight, to struggle against, to achieve their goals; to force, to be violent, to be aggressive, to coerce. And the sannyasin is one who knows that there is no need – life is already going that way: "I have just to be in tune with life. I have just to be a part of this vast orchestra. I have just to become a note in harmony with the whole. I have to surrender." The sannyasin is not a warrior, not a soldier. He is surrendered.

Once it happened...

Mulla Nasruddin had harnessed a kitten to his broken-down Cadillac. When bystanders pointed out that this was absurd, he replied, "You all may think so, but I've got a horsewhip."

There are people who think that just by forcing, anything is possible – just a horsewhip is needed; you just have to do it a little harder. If you are not succeeding, that simply shows that you are not working hard at it – work a little harder. If you are still not succeeding, then you are not putting all your energy – put a little more energy into it. This is the logic of the accidental world.

The essential man knows that it is not a question of putting more energy, it is not a question of fighting at all; it is a question of allowing existence to happen. Nothing is needed on your part to be done...only one thing: a deep trust and surrender.

But sometimes it happens, just like the waving of the blanket by the medicine man. You wave the blanket and something happens. You think it is happening because of the waving of your blanket. Had you waited a little, it would have happened on its own. You simply wasted your energy by waving the blanket.

Sometimes it happens that you have been struggling for something yet it happens – that gives your mind the idea that it has happened "because of my effort." Then you are in a vicious circle. When you fail you think "I have not been making as much effort as needed." When you succeed you think "I have done as much as was needed." But, in fact, things go on happening of their own accord; they don't happen by your effort. Sometimes it is a coincidence that they happen even when you are making an effort.

All that is beautiful, true, and good, simply comes as a grace.

It descends on you. And once some effort succeeds, you are in a mad mess. Then you think, now...

An architect was having a difficult time with Mulla Nasruddin, a prospective home-builder. "But can't you give some idea," he pleaded, "of the general type of house you want to build, Nasruddin?"

"Well," replied the Mulla hesitantly, "all I know is: it must go with an antique doorknob my wife bought the other day."

He has only an antique doorknob and he wants to make a house. The only thing he knows is it must go with the antique doorknob. That's how we are working. A small effort has succeeded – so you have an antique doorknob – now you are trying to create the whole house of life accordingly. You are creating trouble for yourself. And that antique doorknob is also not because of your efforts. It is better to say that it happened in spite of your efforts. Somehow you coincided with the universe.

This is the whole philosophy of the religious man: "I have nothing to do, just to celebrate, just let things happen to me, just dance and sing." It does not mean that a religious man becomes inactive. No. He becomes more active, but in his action there is no effort, there is no strain, there is no violence. It is not that he becomes inactive, dull, lethargic – no. He radiates with energy, he overflows with energy, because all the energy that was being wasted in effort is no longer wasted. He has too much of it, he can share. But now he functions as a vehicle. Now he has given his whole energy to the whole. Now, wherever the whole takes him, he goes. Now he is with the whole and not against it.

Whether you go to a church or to a temple – or not – is irrelevant. If you are with the whole, you are a religious person. Whether you are a Christian or a Hindu or a Mohammedan is irrelevant. If you are with the whole, you are a religious person. And remember this with me: I am not here to convert you to become a Hindu, to become a Mohammedan, to become a Christian. All that nonsense is not for me. I am here to help you to become religious – with no adjective attached to it.

And once you start understanding this, the world takes on a totally new color. Even sometimes there is pain – yet you are understanding. Sometimes it hurts – yes, even then it is not all roses, it cannot be; but you start understanding it. In fact, you start seeing that thorns are there to protect the roses, that night is needed to help the day to be born, that death is needed to refresh life. Once you start understanding, you become positive. Then whatever happens, you can always look deeper into its meaning, its significance.

I was reading a poem:

> The world is a beautiful place
> To be born into,
> If you don't mind happiness
> Not always being
> So very much fun,
> If you don't mind a touch of hell
> Now and then
> Just when everything is fine –
> Because even in heaven
> They don't sing
> All the time.

Even a dancer needs a rest, even a singer needs a rest. Even a happy person needs rest. One cannot remain in one mood continuously, there is no need. When there are so many climates available, why get attached to one? Why not be enriched by all?

A man who has attained his essential center moves on dancing in different situations. Sometimes it is hot, sometimes it is cold; sometimes it is joy, sometimes it is sadness – but now everything brings him some message from the whole. Everything has become a messenger.

This story, today's story, is a very simple story but very significant. And it always happens that significant things are very simple, and simple things are very significant.

> *There was a man of Wei, Tung-Men Wu, who did not grieve when his son died.*
> *His wife said to him:"No one in the world loved his son as much as you did, why do you not grieve now he is dead?"*
> *He answered:"I had no son, and when I had no son I did not grieve. Now that he is dead it is the same as it*

was before, when I had no son. Why should I grieve over him?"

A very simple parable, but tremendously significant, very meaningful. Enter it layer by layer: *There was a man of Wei, Tung-Men Wu, who did not grieve when his son died.* It is very difficult not to grieve when somebody you loved so much has died. It is possible only if you have known something of the essential. It is possible only if you have tasted something of the deathless. It is possible only if you have transcended the accidental. He did not grieve, he was not sad. He was not weeping or crying, he was not broken. He remained just the same as he was.

The wife was disturbed. She said: *"No one in the world loved his son as much as you did, why do you not grieve now he is dead?"* Ordinarily, this is our logic, that if you love a person too much you will grieve too much when he is gone. The logic is fallacious; the logic has a very deep flaw in it. In fact, if you have loved a person really, when he is gone he is gone; you will not grieve much. If you have not loved the person deeply, then you will grieve very much. Try to understand this.

Your father dies, or your mother dies. If you have loved your father totally while he was alive, you will be able to say good-bye to him without any grief – because you loved him. That experience of love was total and fulfilling. Nothing is left undone, nothing is hanging over your head. Whatever was possible has happened; now you can accept it. What more was possible? Even if he had been alive, what more would have been possible? The experience is complete.

Whenever an experience is complete, you are ready to say good-bye very easily. But if you have not loved your father as you always wanted to, you have not been respectful toward him as you always wanted to, you will feel guilty. Now your father is gone. Now there is no way to fulfill your desire; now there is no way to show your respect, your love. Now there is no way. You will feel yourself hanging in the middle, in midair, in a limbo. You will not be at ease; you cannot say good-bye. You will cry and weep and you will be broken, and you will say that you are broken because your father is dead, but the real thing is something else.

You are broken because now the possibility to love him, to respect him, is gone. Now there is no possibility – the doors are closed and you have missed an opportunity. The son will cry more if he has not really loved his father. If he has loved his father, he will be able to accept the fact. Love is very accepting and very understanding.

Once an experience is complete, you can get out of it very easily – you can just slip out of it as the snake slips out of his old skin. If you love a woman and you have been constantly quarreling with her, and it never became a deep satisfaction, and she dies... Now she will haunt; her ghost will haunt you for your whole life. You could not do something that was possible, but now it is no longer possible. Now something incomplete will always be there in the heart, hurting; it will become a wound.

This is the understanding of all the sages, that while you are loving a person, if you love him totally there is going to be no misery. If you love him totally, if you enjoy and delight in him totally, and the person is gone... Of course, one feels a little sad, but it is not grief; one misses a little, but one is capable of remaining centered, one is not distracted.

If you are in love, love totally – so nothing remains hanging. Otherwise, that hanging, incomplete experience, that unlived experience, will haunt you. These unlived experiences go on piling up and they become heavy burdens.

And the problem is that now there is no way – what to do with them? You cannot complete them because the person has disappeared. You cannot drop them because incomplete experiences cannot be dropped. It is just like a ripe fruit drops of its own accord. When it is ripe, it drops; when it is not ripe, it is difficult to drop. Whenever an experience is complete, it is a ripe fruit – it drops of its own accord. It leaves no scar behind, no wound.

The wife says: *"No one in the world loved his son as much as you did, why do you not grieve now he is dead?"* She is giving the argument of the accidental mind. That is the argument of the accidental man: Why don't you grieve? In fact, the accidental man was not really happy while the person was alive, but he becomes very unhappy when the person is gone.

I used to know a woman who was very unhappy with her husband – almost in hell, continuously fighting, quarreling, nagging. The husband started drinking too much just to avoid all this. Then the fight became even more fierce because the wife started fighting against his drinking. It led him to even more drinking. When he was only thirty-six he died – died because of drinking too much.

The woman was never happy. She lived with him for almost seven years, she was never happy. All those seven years I knew them; they were next-door neighbors to me. And always the husband would come with his miseries, and the wife would come with her miseries – I was a silent watcher. Then the husband died and the woman became so sad. Months passed and she was crying and crying, and she was going mad.

One day I went to her, and there was nobody else present so I told her, "Now I can be true to you. Stop this nonsense – because you were never happy with this man. In fact, many times you have told me that if this man dies it will be good. Now he is dead, he has fulfilled your desire. So why are you crying and weeping? I can't see any point in it. Are you missing all those fights? Are you missing all that misery? I cannot see that you are missing the man, because there was nothing in it!"

She was shocked. She had never expected something like that from me or from anybody else. People in such situations expect sympathy. I said, "Stop this nonsense! I know that you were never happy. Now you can be happy! He is no longer there to create any trouble."

She looked at me, shocked. Her tears dried and she said, "It is shocking, but you have made me alert about one thing: I am not missing him at all. I am simply crying and weeping because I could not love him. It is not his death, it is my own missed experience of love. I loved that man, but I could not love. We wasted the whole opportunity in quarreling over futile things. Now I know those things mean nothing. Now that he is gone, I know those things were just trivia. I can't even remember the reasons why we were fighting continuously."

If you love a person totally and the experience is complete, has enriched you, you can say good-bye. Of course, there will be sadness, but there will be no grief. And sadness is natural. It will disappear in time; it is nothing to be worried about. You will miss the person a little while – natural – but you will not be in grief.

The accidental man says if you don't cry when a person is dead, that means you never loved him. That's what the wife of Tung-Men Wu was trying to point out: "You loved him so much. At least you pretended to love him so much, as if nobody has ever loved his son so much. Now what has happened? There is no grief! What type of love is this?" If you ask me, I say it is because he really loved the child. Now that he is gone, he is gone.

Love is understanding. And love is so understanding that not only does it understand life, it understands death also.

He answered: "I had no son, and when I had no son I did not grieve." This is the logic of the essential man. He says: "There was a moment in my life when the son was not there, and I was happy without him. I had known no grief then. Then the son came and I was happy with him. Now that he is gone, I am again in the same situation as before, before he was born. And I was not in grief then, so why should I be in grief now? Again I am in the same situation: the son is not there; I am not a father again. Once I used to be not a father, then I became a father. I am again not a father. Something has happened, disappeared...I am left in the same way as I was before."

It is said about a great sage who was a prime minister: when he was appointed prime minister to a king, he was almost a beggar on the streets. But the news of his wisdom spread, rumors started coming to the palace, and the king started going to him and he was impressed. He was tremendously impressed by the man and his insight – he appointed him as his prime minister.

The beggar came to the palace. The king said, "Now you can drop your robe." Beautiful clothes were ready for him. He was given a good bath; beautiful robes were given to him, ornaments, as befits a prime minister.

Then everybody became intrigued by the fact that in one room he had something like treasure locked. And every day he used to go, unlock the door – he would go alone, he would not allow anybody inside – lock the door again, and he would remain there for at least half an hour, then come out. Everybody became suspicious: What is happening in that room? What does he have in that room? Is there some conspiracy? Is there some secret? And, of course, the king also became interested.

One day the king said, "I would like to come with you into your private room. I could not sleep last night. I continuously worried about what is there."

The prime minister said, "There is nothing. And it is not worthy of your eyes. I will not take you."

The king became even more suspicious. He said, "There seems

to be some danger! I cannot allow this to happen in my palace. You will have to take me in!"

The prime minister said, "If you don't trust me, then I will take you in – but then this will be the end of my prime ministership. Then take my resignation and come into the room. Otherwise, trust me and never ask about the room!"

But the king was really suspicious. He said, "Okay, give your resignation but I am coming into the room."

With his whole court they entered. There was nothing...his old robe, just the old robe hanging on a nail in the room. They looked around, there was nothing – the room was empty. They said, "Why do you come here?"

He said, "Just to see this robe, to remind me that once I was a beggar, and any day I will be a beggar again. Just to remind me so that I don't get too much attached to this prime ministership."

He stepped out of his clothes, took his robe. The king started weeping and crying; he said, "Don't go!"

But he said, "Now, enough is enough. You could not trust me. And when there is no trust there is no point in my being here. I must go." But the sage left the palace the same way he had entered one day. Those ten, twelve years he remained the prime minister meant nothing – that was just an accident.

This is what this man is saying: "I had no son, and when I had no son I did not grieve. I never missed this son when he was not there. When I was not a father, I never missed him, so why now should I miss him? Again the same situation has come back. Now that he is dead, it is the same as it was before when I had no son. Why should I grieve over him?"

This is the way to watch life. Whatever is accidental... You are living in a big house, in a palace – remember that if this palace is taken away from you, there is no point in becoming depressed. Once you were living outside the palace, so again you are under the sky. You become very respectable, and then something happens...you are condemned by the society. What is the point in being worried about it? One day you were not famous at all and you were happy; again you can be happy.

One day you were not in this world. When you were not born, do you remember that you were unhappy in any way? Then why be worried when you die? You will be again in the same state. You were not, and you don't remember any unhappiness. One day you will again disappear; why be worried? You will be again in the same state: you will not be again – at least not in the way that you are here.

This is what Zen people say: Find out your original face – the face that you had before you were born, and the face that will be there when you are dead. Find out the eternal, and don't pay much attention to the accidental.

If you can drop out of the accidental, you have dropped out of the world. There is no need to go anywhere. It is an inner attitude.

Remember: Remain alert that you don't get too much attached to the accidental – and all is accidental except your consciousness. Except your awareness, all is accidental. Pain and pleasure, success and failure, fame and defamation – all is accidental. Only your witnessing consciousness is essential. Stick to it. Get more and more rooted in it. And don't spread your attachment to worldly things.

I don't mean leave them. I don't mean leave your house, leave your wife, leave your children; but remember that it is just an accident that you are together. It is not going to be an eternal state. It has a beginning, it will have an end. Remember that you were happy even before it began, and you will be happy when it has ended. If you can carry this touchstone, you can always judge what is accidental and what is essential.

That which is always is truth. That which is momentary is untrue.

In the East and in the West there is a difference in the definition of truth. In the Western philosophy, truth is equivalent to the real. In the East, truth is equivalent to the eternal...because in the East we say even the momentary is real, real for the moment – but it is not true because it is not eternal. It is just a reflection.

The reflection is also real. You see the moon in the sky and the reflection in the lake; the reflection is also real because it is there. There is a difference between the reflection and no reflection, so it is real. Even a dream is real – because when you dream, it is there. It is real as a dream, but it is real. The only difference between the dream and the waking state is that the dream lasts only for a few moments, the waking state lasts longer. But in the East we have come to the ultimate awakening also. Then this waking state also looks momentary, then this too is dreamlike.

The eternal is true. The temporal is untrue. Both are real. The accidental is also real and the essential is also real, but with the accidental you will remain in misery. And with the essential the doors of bliss open, the doors of *sat chit anand* – of truth, of consciousness, of bliss.

Remember this story in your day-to-day life. Imbibe its impact. If you can remember it, it can become a transforming influence on your life; it can transfigure you. It can help you to reach your center.

Life is only an opportunity to grow, to be, to bloom. Life in itself is empty; unless you are creative you will not be able to fill it with fulfillment. You have a song in your heart to be sung and you have a dance to be danced, but the dance is invisible, and the song – even you have not heard it yet. It is hidden deep down in the innermost core of your being; it has to be brought to the surface, it has to be expressed. That's what is meant by 'self-actualization'. Rare is the person who transforms his life into a growth, who transforms his life into a long journey of self-actualization, who becomes what he was meant to be. In the East we have called that man the Buddha, in the West we have called that man the Christ. The word christ *exactly means what the word* buddha *means: one who has come home.*

The Buddha

> The West has given birth to Aristotle, Nietzsche, Heidegger, Camus, Berdyaev, Marcel and Sartre. Is it going to give birth to buddhas by itself or is a communion with the Eastern consciousness needed?

The buddha-consciousness is neither Eastern nor Western. It has nothing to do with geography or history, it has nothing to do with the mind as such. The mind is Eastern, Western, Indian, Chinese, Japanese, German, but the innermost pure consciousness is simply the pure sky – you cannot identify it with anything because it is unconditioned.

What is East and what is West? – ways of conditioning, different ways of conditioning. What is a Hindu and what is a Jew? – different ways of conditioning. These are names of diseases. Health is neither Eastern nor Western.

A child is born, and immediately the conditioning starts – very subtle are the ways of conditioning. Directly, indirectly, we start pressing the child into a certain mold. He will speak a certain language, and each language has its ways of thinking, each language has its emphasis, its particular direction. That's why sometimes it becomes impossible to translate from one language into another; the other language may not even have words which correspond, the other language may not have looked at reality and life in that way. Life is infinite; the way you look at it is finite – there can be infinite ways of looking at it.

And then the child starts getting colored by the family, by the school, the church, the priest, the parents – and it goes on silently.

Slowly, slowly the whole sky of consciousness is closed; only a small window, an aperture, is left open. That aperture is Indian, English, American. That aperture is Hindu, Jaina, Buddhist. That aperture is Eastern, Western.

To realize buddhahood is to regain the consciousness that you brought with your birth. That uncontaminated purity, that original face without any masks, that innocence is buddhahood. So buddhahood cannot be Eastern or Western; it is transcendental.

You may be surprised that when a child grows up in a family... and each child has to grow in a family. It is almost a must, there is no other way; some kind of family is needed. Even if it is a commune it will have its own limitations, it may be a kibbutz but it will have its own limitations. And there is no way to bring up a child without a certain nourishing surrounding. That nourishing surrounding is a must, without it the child cannot survive; the child has to be looked after, but the child has to pay for it. It is not simple, it is very complex. The child has to continuously adjust himself to the family because the family is "right," the father is "right," the mother is "right." They are powerful people – the child is helpless. He has to depend on them, he has to look up to them, he has to follow them. Right or wrong is not the question; the child has to become a shadow, an imitator.

That's what Hinduism is, Christianity is, that's what the Eastern and Western mind is. And it is very subtle; the child may never become aware of it because it is not done in one day, it goes on so slowly – just like the water falling from the mountain, falling and falling and falling, and it destroys the rocks, and the stones disappear.

The child has to adjust in many ways. That adjustment makes him false, inauthentic, makes him untrue – untrue to his own being. Now psychologists have discovered that if a certain child proves to be stupid, it may not be so because no child is born stupid. It may be just the whole surrounding, the family, that he had to adjust to. If the father is too intellectual, the child will have to behave in a stupid way to keep a balance. If the child behaves in an intelligent way, the father is, in a subtle way, angry. He cannot tolerate an intelligent child, he never tolerates anybody who is trying to be more intelligent than him. He will force the child to remain inferior, notwithstanding what he goes on saying. And the child will learn the trick of behaving like a fool because when he behaves like a fool everything goes okay, everything is perfectly okay. The father may show his displeasure on the surface, but deep down he is satisfied. He always likes fools around him; surrounded by fools, he is the most intelligent person.

Because of this, over hundreds of years women have learned a trick: they never try to be intellectual – the husband won't like it. Not that they are not intelligent, they are as intelligent as men – but they have to learn. Have you not watched it? If the wife is more educated, the husband feels a little bad about it. No man wants to marry a woman who is more educated than him, more famous than him. Not only that, but in small things too: if the woman is taller, no man wants to marry her. Maybe it is just because of this that women have decided on a biological level also not to become too tall: there may be some kind of psychological reason in it – otherwise you will not get a husband. If you are too intelligent you will not get a husband. The woman has to pretend that she always remains a baby, childish, so that the husband can feel good that the woman leans on him.

In a family, the child comes into a ready-made situation. Everything is already there; he has to fit himself into it, he has to adjust to it. He cannot be himself; if he tries to be himself he always gets into trouble and he starts feeling guilty. He has to adjust – whatever the cost. Survival is the most important thing, the first thing, other things are secondary. So each child has to adjust to the family, to the parent, to geography, to history, to the idiosyncrasies of the people around him, to all kinds of prejudices, stupid beliefs, superstitions. By the time you become aware or you become a little bit independent, you are so conditioned, the conditioning has gone so deep in the blood and the bones and the marrow, that you cannot get out of it.

What is buddhahood? Buddhahood is getting out of this whole conditioning. A buddha is one who lives as a whole, as an organic whole. Buddha consciousness is transcendental consciousness. It has nothing to do with East or West.

What are the characteristics of an enlightened being?

An enlightened being simply means a man who has no longer any questions left in his life, everything is solved. An enlightened man means a man who is constantly in the same state of silence, peace and contentment, whatever happens on the outside: success or failure, pain or pleasure, life or death.

An enlightened man means a man who has experienced something that you are also capable of, but you have not tried it. He is full of light, full of joy, full of ecstasy, twenty-four hours a day. He is almost a drunkard, drunk with the divine. His life is a song, his life is a dance, his life is a rejoicing. His presence is a blessing.

And if you want to know him, you have to be with him. You cannot watch him from the outside, you have to come close. You have to come in a state of intimacy. You have to join his caravan, you have to hold his hand. You have to feed on him, and you have to allow, to let him enter your heart. But from the outside, please don't try to find any characteristic; these are all inner experiences.

But some indications can always be given. In the proximity of the enlightened being you will feel a certain magnetic force, a tremendous attraction, a charismatic center. Out of your fear you may not come close. It is dangerous to come close to an enlightened man, because you can come close but then you cannot go away. Coming close is risky. It is only for gamblers, not for businessmen.

Have you read Zorba the Greek*? Read it! Zorba says to his boss, "There is something missing in you, boss. A touch of madness! Unless you cut the string, you will never really live."*
A little madness gives you dimensions, gives you poetry, and gives you enough courage to be happy in this unhappy world.

I would like you to be Zorba the Greek and Gautam the Buddha together, simultaneously. Less than that won't do. Zorba represents the earth with all its flowers and greenery and mountains and rivers and oceans. Buddha represents the sky with all its stars and clouds, and the rainbows. The sky without the earth will be empty. The sky cannot laugh without the earth. The earth without the sky will be dead. Both together – and a dance comes into existence. The earth and the sky dancing together – and there is laughter, there is joy, there is celebration.

Zorba the Buddha

Can you explain more about what you mean by "Zorba the Buddha"?

My rebel, my new man, is Zorba the Buddha.

Mankind has lived believing either in the reality of the soul and the illusoriness of matter, or in the reality of matter and the illusoriness of the soul.

You can divide the humanity of the past into the spiritualists and the materialists. But nobody has bothered to look at the reality of man. He is both together. He is neither just spirituality – he is not just consciousness – nor is he just matter. He is a tremendous harmony between matter and consciousness.

Or perhaps matter and consciousness are not two things, but only two aspects of one reality: matter is the outside of consciousness, and consciousness is the interiority of matter. But there has not been a single philosopher, sage, or religious mystic in the past who has declared this unity; they were all in favor of dividing man, calling one side real and the other side unreal. This has created an atmosphere of schizophrenia all over the earth.

You cannot live just as a body. That's what Jesus means when he says, "Man cannot live by bread alone" – but this is only half the truth. You cannot live just as consciousness alone, you cannot live without bread either. You have two dimensions of your being and both dimensions have to be fulfilled, given equal opportunity for growth. But the past has been either in favor of one and against the other, or in favor of the other and against the first one.

Man as a totality has not been accepted. This has created

misery, anguish, and a tremendous darkness; a night that has lasted for thousands of years, that seems to have no end. If you listen to the body, you condemn yourself; if you don't listen to the body, you suffer – you are hungry, you are poor, you are thirsty. If you listen to consciousness only, your growth will be lopsided: your consciousness will grow but your body will shrink, and the balance will be lost. And in the balance is your health, in the balance is your wholeness, in the balance is your joy, your song, your dance.

The West has chosen to listen to the body, and has become completely deaf as far as the reality of consciousness is concerned. The ultimate result is great science, great technology, an affluent society, a richness of things mundane, worldly. And amidst all this abundance, a poor man without a soul, completely lost – not knowing who he is, not knowing why he is, feeling almost an accident or a freak of nature. Unless consciousness grows with the richness of the material world, the body – matter – becomes too heavy and the soul becomes too weak. You are too burdened by your own inventions, your own discoveries. Rather than creating a beautiful life for you, they create a life which is felt by all the intelligentsia of the West as not worth living.

The East has chosen consciousness and has condemned matter and everything material, the body included, as maya, as illusory, as a mirage in a desert which only appears but has no reality in itself. The East has created a Gautam Buddha, a Mahavira, a Patanjali, a Kabir, a Farid, a Raidas – a long line of people with great consciousness, with great awareness. But it has also created millions of poor people, hungry, starving, dying like dogs – with not enough food, no pure water to drink, not enough clothes, not enough shelter.

A strange situation.... In the West, every six months they have to sink billions and billions of dollars' worth of milk products and other foodstuff in the ocean, because it is surplus. They don't want to overload their warehouses, they don't want to lower their prices and destroy their economic structure. On the one hand, in Ethiopia one thousand people were dying every day, and at the same time the European Common Market was destroying so much food that the cost of destroying it was millions of dollars. That is not the cost of the food; it is the cost of taking it to the ocean, and throwing it into the ocean. Who is responsible for this situation?

The richest man in the West is searching for his soul and finding himself hollow, without any love, only lust; without any prayer, only parrot-like words that he has been taught in the Sunday schools. He has no religiousness, no feeling for other human beings, no reverence for life, for birds, for trees, for animals – destruction is so easy.

Hiroshima and Nagasaki would not have happened if man were not thought to be just matter. So many nuclear weapons would not have been piled up if man had been thought to be a hidden God, a hidden splendor; not to be destroyed but to be discovered, not to be destroyed but to be brought into the light – a temple of God. But if man is just matter, just chemistry, physics, a skeleton covered with skin, then with death everything dies, nothing remains. That's why it becomes possible for an Adolf Hitler to kill six million people, without a hitch. If all people are just matter, there is no question of even thinking twice.

The West has lost its soul, its interiority. Surrounded by meaninglessness, boredom, anguish, it is not finding itself. All the success of science is proving of no use because the house is full of everything, but the master of the house is missing. Here, in the East, the master is alive but the house is empty. It is difficult to rejoice with hungry stomachs, with sick bodies, with death surrounding you; it is impossible to meditate. So, unnecessarily, we have been losers. All our saints, and all our philosophers, spiritualists and materialists both, are responsible for this immense crime against man.

Zorba the Buddha is the answer. It is the synthesis of matter and soul. It is a declaration that there is no conflict between matter and consciousness, that we can be rich on both sides. We can have everything that the world can provide, that science and technology can produce, and we can still have everything that a Buddha, a Kabir, a Nanak finds in his inner being – the flowers of ecstasy, the fragrance of godliness, the wings of ultimate freedom.

Zorba the Buddha is the new man, is the rebel.

His rebellion consists of destroying the schizophrenia of man, destroying the dividedness – destroying spirituality as against materialism, and destroying materialism as against spirituality. It is a manifesto that body and soul are together: that existence is full of spirituality, that even mountains are alive, that even trees are sensitive, that the whole existence is both – or perhaps just one energy expressing itself in two ways, as matter and as consciousness. When energy is purified it expresses itself as consciousness; when energy is crude, unpurified, dense, it appears as matter. But the whole existence is nothing but an energyfield.

This is my experience, it is not my philosophy. And this is supported by modern physics and its researches: existence is energy.

We can allow man to have both the worlds together. He need not renounce this world to get the other world, nor has he to deny the other world to enjoy this world. In fact, to have only one world while you are capable of having both is to be unnecessarily poor.

Zorba the Buddha is the richest possibility. He will live his nature to its utmost and he will sing songs of this earth. He will not betray the earth, and he will not betray the sky either. He will claim all that this earth has – all the flowers, all the pleasures – and he will also claim all the stars of the sky. He will claim the whole existence as his home.

The man of the past was poor because he divided existence. The new man, my rebel, Zorba the Buddha, claims the whole world as his home. All that it contains is for us, and we have to use it in every possible way – without any guilt, without any conflict, without any choice. Choicelessly enjoy all that matter is capable of, and rejoice in all that consciousness is capable of.

Be a Zorba, but don't stop there. Go on moving toward being a Buddha. Zorba is half, Buddha is half.

There is an ancient story:

In a forest nearby to a city there lived two beggars. Naturally they were enemies to each other, as all professionals are – two doctors, two professors, two saints. One was blind and one was lame, and both were very competitive; the whole day they were competing with each other in the city.

But one night their huts caught fire, because the whole forest was on fire. The blind man could run out, but he could not see where to run, he could not see where the fire had not yet spread. The lame man could see that there are still possibilities of getting out of this fire, but he could not run out. The fire was too fast, too wild, so the lame man could only see his death coming.

They realized that they needed each other. The lame man had a sudden realization, "The other man can run, the blind man can run, and I can see." They forgot all their competition. In such a critical moment, when both were facing death, each necessarily forgot all stupid enmities. They created a great synthesis; they agreed that the blind man would carry the lame man on his shoulders and they would function as one man – the lame man could see, and the blind man could run. They saved their lives. And because they saved each other's lives they became friends; for the first time they dropped their antagonism.

Zorba is blind – he cannot see, but he can dance, he can sing, he can rejoice. The Buddha can see, but he can only see. He is pure eyes, just clarity and perception, but he cannot dance; he is crippled, he cannot sing, he cannot rejoice.

It is time. The world is a wildfire; everybody's life is in danger. The meeting of Zorba and Buddha can save the whole humanity. Their meeting is the only hope. Buddha can contribute consciousness, clarity, eyes to see beyond, eyes to see that which is almost invisible. Zorba can give his whole being to Buddha's vision and let it not remain just a dry vision, but make it a dancing, rejoicing, ecstatic way of life.

I am giving Buddha energy to dance, and I am giving Zorba eyes to see beyond the skies to faraway destinies of existence and evolution. My rebel is nobody other than Zorba the Buddha.

About Osho

Osho's unique contribution to the understanding of who we are defies categorization. Mystic and scientist, a rebellious spirit whose sole interest is to alert humanity to the urgent need to discover a new way of living. To continue as before is to invite threats to our very survival on this unique and beautiful planet.

His essential point is that only by changing ourselves, one individual at a time, can the outcome of all our "selves" – our societies, our cultures, our beliefs, our world – also change. The doorway to that change is meditation.

Osho the scientist has experimented and scrutinized all the approaches of the past and examined their effects on the modern human being and responded to their shortcomings by creating a new starting point for the hyperactive 21st Century mind: OSHO Active Meditations.

Once the agitation of a modern lifetime has started to settle, "activity" can melt into "passivity," a key starting point of real meditation. To support this next step, Osho has transformed the ancient "art of listening" into a subtle contemporary methodology: the OSHO Talks. Here words become music, the listener discovers who is listening, and the awareness moves from what is being heard to the individual doing the listening. Magically, as silence arises, what needs to be heard is understood directly, free from the distraction of a mind that can only interrupt and interfere with this delicate process.

These thousands of talks cover everything from the individual quest for meaning to the most urgent social and political issues facing society today. Osho's books are not written but are transcribed from audio and video recordings of these extemporaneous talks to international audiences. As he puts it, "So remember: whatever I am saying is not just for you...I am talking also for the future generations."

Osho has been described by *The Sunday Times* in London as one of the "1000 Makers of the 20th Century" and by American author Tom Robbins as "the most dangerous man since Jesus

Christ." *Sunday Mid-Day* (India) has selected Osho as one of ten people – along with Gandhi, Nehru and Buddha – who have changed the destiny of India.

About his own work Osho has said that he is helping to create the conditions for the birth of a new kind of human being. He often characterizes this new human being as "Zorba the Buddha" – capable both of enjoying the earthy pleasures of a Zorba the Greek and the silent serenity of a Gautama the Buddha.

Running like a thread through all aspects of Osho's talks and meditations is a vision that encompasses both the timeless wisdom of all ages past and the highest potential of today's (and tomorrow's) science and technology.

Osho is known for his revolutionary contribution to the science of inner transformation, with an approach to meditation that acknowledges the accelerated pace of contemporary life. His unique OSHO Active Meditations™ are designed to first release the accumulated stresses of body and mind, so that it is then easier to take an experience of stillness and thought-free relaxation into daily life.

Two autobiographical works by the author are available:
Autobiography of a Spiritually Incorrect Mystic,
St Martins Press, New York (book and eBook)
Glimpses of a Golden Childhood,
OSHO Media International, Pune, India (book and eBook)

OSHO International Meditation Resort

Each year the Meditation Resort welcomes thousands of people from more than 100 countries. The unique campus provides an opportunity for a direct personal experience of a new way of living – with more awareness, relaxation, celebration and creativity. A great variety of around-the-clock and around-the-year program options are available. Doing nothing and just relaxing is one of them!

All of the programs are based on Osho's vision of "Zorba the Buddha" – a qualitatively new kind of human being who is able *both* to participate creatively in everyday life *and* to relax into silence and meditation.

Location

Located 100 miles southeast of Mumbai in the thriving modern city of Pune, India, the OSHO International Meditation Resort is a holiday destination with a difference. The Meditation Resort is spread over 28 acres of spectacular gardens in a beautiful tree-lined residential area.

OSHO Meditations

A full daily schedule of meditations for every type of person includes both traditional and revolutionary methods, and particularly the OSHO Active Meditations™. The daily meditation program takes place in what must be the world's largest meditation hall, the OSHO Auditorium.

OSHO Multiversity

Individual sessions, courses and workshops cover everything from creative arts to holistic health, personal transformation, relationship and life transition, transforming meditation into a lifestyle for life and work, esoteric sciences, and the "Zen" approach to sports and recreation. The secret of the OSHO Multiversity's success lies in the fact that all its programs are combined with meditation, supporting the understanding that as human beings we are far more than the sum of our parts.

OSHO Basho Spa

The luxurious Basho Spa provides for leisurely open-air swimming surrounded by trees and tropical green. The uniquely styled, spacious Jacuzzi, the saunas, gym, tennis courts...all these are enhanced by their stunningly beautiful setting.

Cuisine

A variety of different eating areas serve delicious Western, Asian and Indian vegetarian food – most of it organically grown especially for the Meditation Resort. Breads and cakes are baked in the resort's own bakery.

Night life

There are many evening events to choose from – dancing being at the top of the list! Other activities include full-moon meditations beneath the stars, variety shows, music performances and meditations for daily life.

Facilities

You can buy all of your basic necessities and toiletries in the Galleria. The Multimedia Gallery sells a large range of OSHO media products. There is also a bank, a travel agency and a Cyber Café on-campus. For those who enjoy shopping, Pune provides all the options, ranging from traditional and ethnic Indian products to all of the global brand-name stores.

Accommodation

You can choose to stay in the elegant rooms of the OSHO Guesthouse, or for longer stays on campus you can select one of the OSHO Living-In programs. Additionally there is a plentiful variety of nearby hotels and serviced apartments.

www.osho.com/meditationresort
www.osho.com/guesthouse
www.osho.com/livingin

For More Information

www.OSHO.com

a comprehensive multi-language website including a magazine, OSHO Books, OSHO Talks in audio and video formats, the OSHO Library text archive in English and Hindi and extensive information about OSHO Meditations. You will also find the program schedule of the OSHO Multiversity and information about the OSHO International Meditation Resort.

http://OSHO.com/AllAboutOSHO
http://OSHO.com/Resort
http://OSHO.com/Shop
http://www.youtube.com/OSHO
http://www.Twitter.com/OSHO
http://www.facebook.com/pages/OSHO.International

To contact OSHO International Foundation:
www.osho.com/oshointernational,
oshointernational@oshointernational.com

250 · 3 · 2 = 1500 + 450.5
2250
1500
3750